The Freedom to

BIRTHING IN PEACE

NADRA DYAN COHENS

ISBN: 978-0692464687

Scripture quotations from the Holy Bible, New King James Version,
New English Standard Version, New International Version and
Message Bible. Used by permission of Tyndale House Publishers, Inc.,
Carol Stream, Illinois 60188. All rights reserved.

Contributions by Channing D. Cohens, Contributions by Deborah D.
Walker, Edited by Deborah D. Walker, Designed by Karolyne Roberts,
Photography by Anthony D. Thomas

For information on bulk orders, contact us at
everydaymothersintuition@gmail.com.

ACKNOWLEDGEMENTS

This book would not be possible if it was not for key people in my life. I give all glory to God for He poured knowledge, wisdom and understanding into my heart. He birthed in me a heart to want to serve and encourage a particular group of people—wives, mothers and children. I am humbled to allow Him to use me in such a way. However, I couldn't have completed it without the endless love and support from some important people in my life.

To My Husband and Best Friend:

Channing, the Lord couldn't have blessed me with a more awesome man to live this journey called life. Our storybook has been perfectly imperfect but that is why I cherish it because you have been the co-author with me the entire way. You have covered me in countless times in prayer, in acts of service, encouragement, and support. Thank you for choosing to love me as Christ loves the church; Thank you for being so patient and kind; Thank you for being my covering and backbone. I love you forever!

To My Children:

Azaria, Caleb, and Cayden, I thank God for each and every one of you. You all have been an instrumental part in writing this book. Each of you continues to touch my heart and allows the Lord to use you to school the "Teacher." You have inspired me to be overall a better mother and your first example of what a Godly woman should be. Thank you for loving me in each of your unique ways. Azaria, I love your sweet and quiet spirit that exudes compassion to all. Caleb, I love your inquisitive nature and quiet confidence that is firm in not allowing anyone to move you. My baby Cayden, I love your boldness and explosive personality, which I know God will use in a mighty way. I am eternally grateful and honored to be the person that each one of you calls 'Mommy.'

Christian, although you did not come from my womb, I am honored to have you as a bonus child in my life. I will never be able to, nor will I try to, take the place of your mother. However, I am humbled to cover you in prayer every day, every month and year. Your physical presence is not with us every day. But you are and will always be a part of our little family that will continue to honor God, with our whole hearts, by serving others. I cannot wait to see how God uses your life for His glory.

To my Heart, my 'Mommy':

Mom, you have served everyone that you encounter with love, grace, and compassion through excellence. Your love for serving is not only admirable but inspires others, not to mention me, to give more. I am eternally grateful that God chose you to form me in your womb. I am honored that I have been able to see your example for my thirty-three years of life. I thank you for always being there and being so patient, kind and the best 'Ama' ever to my children. Channing and I love you. Our family calls you 'Blessed!'

To my Best Friend and Brother:

Heather and Cornelius, you both have been an instrumental part of my adulthood and walk with Christ. Channing and I are forever grateful for your friendship and sisterhood/brotherhood. I thank you for being so supportive through this entire process of carrying out what God has called me to do. It is such a blessing to see you both walk boldly in your callings, which has inspired me and countless others to do the same. I look forward to continuing to reciprocate the same love that you continue to give to us. I love you both dearly!

Thank you to my godparents, my family, "siblings," best friends, and church family for loving and covering me in prayer daily. I love you all!

Contents

PRELUDE

10:01 p.m.

Am I in labor? I think I'm in labor…If I have another contraction in the next 5 to 10 minutes, I will know it's the real thing.

10:08 p.m.

Okay, this is it.

"Mom, I'm in labor… "

"Nadra, no you're not."

I'm pretty sure that I am though. (I'm dumbfounded by her response.)

"You're probably having a Braxton Hicks."

"Okay, Mom. I'll start timing my contractions then."

10:14 p.m.

Okay, that's another one; I'll wait for another one and then I'll tell her again.

10:21 p.m.

"Mom, this is the third contraction that I've had now. They are about 7 minutes apart."

"Wow, okay. Your bag is still not packed, right?"

"Right. It's not packed."

"Okay. I'll go upstairs and back your bag."

10:27 p.m.

"Mom, that's another one."

Now I'm standing up and swaying side to side.

Mom leaves the unfinished bag and runs down the stairs.

"You said you had another one? Okay, let me quickly finish up packing your bag."

10:32 p.m.

"Moooommmmmmmmmmmm!!!

I remember that night like it was yesterday. I had no clue what to expect. I knew that I wanted to have a natural delivery, free of pain medication. Even as a first-time mother at 21 years of age, I knew that it would not be an ideal option for me or my baby. However, everything that I had learned in my childbirth class at the hospital flew out the window. I was overwhelmed with sadness and consumed with fear. My thoughts were filled with panic and anxiety. In reality this wasn't a sudden onslaught of emotion. It was there brewing quietly beneath the surface throughout my entire childbearing experience.

Webster's definition of childbearing is "The process of conceiving, being pregnant with, and giving birth to

13

children." Over the nine months of my pregnancy, I recall being consumed with thoughts of the unknown during the labor and delivery. Forget about the general role of motherhood, my lack of confidence, and the thought of an actual baby coming out of my vagina overwhelmed me. The unknown and intense thoughts overtook me and fear took on a life of its own in my entire being.

Could I actually follow through and complete the goal to have a natural delivery without any intervention? My mom said that she had a natural delivery, but what did that look like thirty years ago? The only thing that I had as a reference point was from watching deliveries on reality shows and movies that showed a three second flick of a mother in labor. Shows that dramatized a beautiful and natural experience depicted it with a dramatic roller coaster ride of emotions along with heightened fear of the unknown of their baby's birth. It was with this mindset that fear continued to flourish inside of me. The seeds of fear continued to be planted through conversations with relatives, friends, co-workers, and random people who had my ear throughout my pregnancy.

After rededicating my life to Christ, I felt strongly that there had to be some advantage, something different about being a Christian and pregnant. When my husband and I received confirmation that we were pregnant with our first child together, I was determined not to have the same experience that I had several years ago. I was also curious about why so many people in the Body of Christ embraced and accepted fear in childbearing.

Webster's dictionary defines peace as "a freedom from disquieting or oppressive thoughts or emotions." If our goal as Christians is to remain in peace, then how can we allow our minds to be cluttered with the world's concept of childbearing? When our peace is under attack, it's time to do some mental spring cleaning! God blesses you with the ability to carry a child, so His goal is not for you to fulfill His will by sentencing you to a lifetime of turmoil. He desires for us to live a life of holiness, love, and peace through Jesus Christ.

It is my prayer that you would receive conviction and healing regarding childbearing through the words that the Holy Spirit gave me to share in this book.

CHAPTER 1

SETTING VISION:

PREGNANCY, BIRTH, AND

YOUR ROLE AS MOTHER

Hope deferred makes the heart sick,
But when the desire comes, it is a tree of life.
Proverbs 13:12, NKJV

I always had a curiosity and interest in babies. The joy and innocence of little ones captured me at a young age. Any opportunity I had, I'd spend around babies. Whether it was at a family function, being a mom's helper, or babysitting while parents had a date night, it was just me enjoying the newness of life. It was fascinating to watch a child stare in amazement at the opening and closing of his hand or seeing a little one become aware that an object exists even when it cannot be seen, or hearing the first sweet babbles being recognized by a baby as her own.

It was always my desire to have more than one child, but I realized that in order to have those children, I knew I had to endure childbearing. The thought of the birth experience seemed so natural yet at the same time so intimidating. Interesting that those thoughts could exist simultaneously; but we live in a world of paradoxes. Life is celebrated but in the same vein the process to birth a child is often filled with such fear.

We love to go through the fun and the novelty of creating a baby registry, planning the most ornate nursery, or picking out the perfect outfit to wear for a maternity photo shoot. But we do not give the same care and thought to preparing ourselves spiritually or physically to go through the entirety of pregnancy and childbirth. The moment that I found out I was pregnant with my daughter, I knew that I had to make some adjustments and do things right. But what did "right" mean? I was so young and naïve at that time. Even when I was so far away from pursuing the will of God for my life, He was chasing me and downloading the desires of my heart that are true to this day.

1 Corinthians 2:12 states that we have the spirit of God and not of this world. Therefore, we have the ability to understand the things that God gives us. We have been set apart for His good. If we proclaim this to be true, than how can we as women of God continue to think the way the world does regarding childbearing?

The scenario is probably familiar to you. You decide to purchase and take a pregnancy test because your menstrual cycle is late. Your body longs to go into slumber at the drop of a hat and there are those bouts of queasiness. After the longest few minutes ever, your eyes widen at the sight of the positive sign on the pregnancy test stick. Whether your reaction is excitement, shock, or 'not now!,' reality sets in and the adventure begins.

Life has already started blossoming inside your womb before your mind catches up to that reality. Then the avalanche of thoughts comes crashing in. Am I equipped to be a mother? Do we have enough money to support a child? What will our priorities be in raising our child? What school will he attend? What influences do we want surrounding our child? I guarantee you there will be a plethora of questions that will swirl around in your head; some warranted and others to be dismissed.

Right off the bat, you will naturally want whatever is the best for your child. We often seek the opinions of professionals, those people in our lives whose words we value, or sometimes we take the advice of those who simply have a listening ear. It is important before you seek anyone's advice that you get an understanding of what God has to say about childbearing and seek wisdom on how pregnancy and childbirth was designed to function.

When your pregnancy is confirmed, this is a critical time to clear your mind of all the outside voices and focus on what you believe childbirth will be for you. Some of you may be on the journey for a second, third, or fourth time. However, just as each child is unique in makeup and personality; so is each pregnancy. Indeed, there might be some similarities and symptoms that you have endured previously, but to presume that your new pregnancy is going to have the same highs and lows robs you of experiencing the uniqueness of each little gift God gives you.

Your pregnancy is an introduction to motherhood and ultimately the journey towards establishing a relationship with your child. When you are becoming acquainted with a new friend, you are not going to necessarily have the same level of intimacy that you have with other longtime friends. There are a multitude of variables that come into play: how and where you met, the common likes or dislikes you share, or memories you've made with one another. Similarly with your pregnancy, you will need to take your time to acclimate and take ownership of the new life that is growing inside of you. You will also need to embrace the way your body is evolving and consider this a season when you are set apart.

Genetics can definitely play a role in how your pregnancy progresses. However, it is not the period at the end of a sentence nor is it a make or break factor. It is rather a variable; and we know that variables are subject to change. There are so many different symptoms that may be surfacing daily. Still, it is important to refocus and realize that this new season that you are about to embark on is what you make of it. In this season, as with life in general, there are times when you will experience hardships, pain, tests, and trials. These moments are often opportunities to show us where we have placed our trust. This is why you can rely on the words Jesus shared with His disciples in John 16:33 (ESV), "...that in me you may have peace. In the world you will have tribulation. But take heart; I have overcome the world."

There will be times when you will not feel comfortable. I knew that my body was designed to grow, stretch, and adapt for the growth of my child. I knew that it would not be an adjustment for my comfort. I had to decide how I was going to experience the ability to carry my child, which so many women hope and pray to experience. Believe it or not, your childbearing days will pass in a flash before your eyes. You can have an experience full of complaints and murmuring or you can let go and make the most of each passing day, week, and month.

When I decided that I was going to be intentional about a natural delivery for my children, it was not because I was seeking praise or accolades. I remembered the negative impression that my first pregnancy had on me. Although there are some gaps in my recollection during my pregnancy and childbirth experience, I can recall coping through moments of helplessness and sadness. I had no choice but to press through feelings of hopelessness, desperation, and ultimately anxiety during my daughter's birth. I just wanted it to be over. Every time I think back to that moment in time, I grieve for the young woman that I was then.

I was married at the time of my next pregnancy and I wanted my outward man to reflect my inward man. Thus, it was my goal to experience my pregnancy free of fear and fully in peace and the only way I was going to accomplish that was to guard my heart daily. This would require me to seek peace and pursue it with all of my being, while rejecting anything that was contrary to it.

A woman can say that she wants to lose weight with such sincerity. But if she doesn't carry out a plan and put it into action, then it is just an unfilled desire. Progress would be obvious if she started to consume healthy foods and implement an exercise routine. Likewise, I had to learn that my conviction to enjoy my pregnancy and to birth my children naturally would have to be carried out with a plan of action.

The first step was to identify what might deter me from having a peaceful childbirth. This required me to be really honest with myself and get rid of any and all excuses. The moment I was able to verbalize that fear was an issue, I was motivated to focus on renewing my mind with the Word of God so that I was spiritually prepared. Many women suppress their feelings of fear about childbearing because they want so desperately to feel like they have it altogether. But then the same woman will run to her girlfriends who have no filter and who are quick to share the horrors of their pregnancies and how painful childbirth was for them.

My ability to overcome in this area was going to require me to be diligent in reading, listening, and consuming anything and everything that lined up with God's Word from the moment that I arose in the morning to the moment that my head hit the pillow at night. I knew that nothing would prosper if my mindset was not changed from the experience of my first pregnancy. This meant sacrificing and letting go of time spent with certain friends or family members. It meant even changing doctors when one would make unnecessary commentary or speculations regarding my low-risk pregnancy that was not relevant to my health or the health of my child. My adjustments meant literally changing the channel of my favorite television show with a character complaining about her pregnancy or the one with a woman screaming uncontrollably on the hospital bed.

I knew that these personal adjustments would seem extreme to some, but I didn't want to succumb to fear of the unknown and give up on the possibility that my childbearing experience could be different. If I didn't endure the process in pregnancy and conquer fear during childbirth, I would ultimately have to accept failure to execute my plan to birth my children naturally. Of course, there were other concerns and questions regarding my pregnancy and my child. But regardless of the information that I had received, the consequences to neglect the process of growth would hinder me beyond childbearing. I knew what my shortcomings were, so I had to be aggressive about moving all distractions from my life. This would ensure that my focus remained on God, so that I would receive strength and power throughout the process.

As born again Christians, our main objective is to be set apart from the world. There are some people with the religious mentality that you can customize the Bible to fit your lifestyle. However, God has given us liberty to live a righteous life full of power, love, and peace. Yet, the Body of Christ is tempted with making exceptions in the area of pregnancy and childbirth.

Women and men alike are notorious for blaming Eve for every minor and traumatic event pertaining to their childbearing experience. I understand that when you are pregnant for the first time, you do not know what to expect. You are searching for all of the answers on how to make things more comfortable, how to endure, what to expect in the weeks and months ahead, and generally wanting all the answers to the questions about the journey of motherhood. However, motherhood is not a sprint, but rather a marathon.

If you understand that pregnancy is your introduction to motherhood, you have to realize you cannot blaze through the process. As a Christian, it will require you to use a hefty dose of wisdom while being Spirit-led in all that you do. I can tell you that you are not going to get all of your questions answered by a professional, a relative, or a friend. Those concerns that toy with you will not be instantly relieved by surfing the Internet or leafing through a book. It will require you to be on your face before God daily, while continuing to develop and ripen the fruit of the spirit such as joy, patience, and self-control.

This journey towards motherhood does not start when your child is born, but rather when he is conceived. Thus, it is imperative to understand the notion that it is never too early to start preparing for motherhood. Whether you are single or newly married, preparation can start today.

Motherhood is an extension of the acts of service that you share with your husband. It is actually amplified because your children rely on you for their every need. The heart of a servant does not look at how someone can cater to her life; but rather how can she add value to others. So, what do you believe you are supposed to add to your child's life? Your child is not going to measure your worth by how much you can provide for them financially or even how much you impact them by your knowledge of the Bible. I am not saying that you do not need to provide for them financially or spiritually. However, your child is going to feel validated and empowered by the love that you show them through Jesus Christ. This will all be relayed and determined by how much you invest in them. Your investment in them as a Christian is going to be the result of having an understanding, revelation, and application of the Word of God to your life first.

Soon you will have a sweet, huggable baby with soft plump legs to squeeze, and chubby, round cheeks to caress. But your little dumpling will not be cradled in your arms for very long.

Before you know it, you will have a child who will begin to take baby steps to maturing into the person he was predestined to become. This child will have feelings, thoughts, character, strengths, and inadequacies—which will all play a role in his/her purpose. However, those details can still be influenced. Your role is vital to molding or shaping him. *Train up a child in the way he should go: and when he is old, he will not depart from it* (Proverbs 22:6, ESV).

Children are masters of observation, especially during the formative years. Early on, children are watching and studying everything in their surroundings. Some habits that children have are innate but others are learned over time. They begin develop behaviors and attitudes which become a part of their make-up. My baby boy may not have an opinion about the respect that I give to his father. However, I am daily providing a mirror to reflect how his future wife should treat him. Likewise, if I were to disrespect my husband in front of our daughter, this would give her permission to think it is okay for her behave the same way. If this is an ongoing habit, this will allow her to formulate a belief that it is okay to talk out of character to her future husband.

My husband and I have set a goal to always walk through our conversations in love and conflict in peace. So even in a moment of a heated discussion, we can show our daughter, through our example, a healthy resolution to our disagreements. This will help her to understand the dynamics of being in a marriage and how to conduct herself in everyday life. Your example in your everyday activities will speak volumes to your child. The words that come from your mouth will have no bearing if they are contradictory to what he sees you doing on a regular basis.

Each stage of the journey has its own set of obstacles and challenges, but it also has its own set of rewards as well. It is a true privilege and honor to accept the role of motherhood. Are you willingly and wholeheartedly ready to accept all that comes with being responsible for another one of God's treasures? Just think God entrusted *you* with your precious child(ren) to grow into worshippers who will build up and edify His kingdom. I don't know about you but that in itself is very humbling to me. It may appear to be a daunting task. But don't think that God has set you up for failure or to grapple with a challenge without any assistance.

In most cases, you will have your husband and leader of your household to guide your family to fulfill the vision that is set for your little community. This will take some of the load off of your shoulders. However, just like everything in life, your husband cannot rescue you, solve every problem, and mend every wound for you and your children. This is the reason we have a Savior! He, above anyone, can make things whole and complete in your life.

I can recall being so overwhelmed in the first year of marriage and having a new baby. It meant scheduling and preparing for our then 8-year-old to participate in her routine of school and other activities; meeting the needs of the baby; finding a way to pursue my purpose while meeting the obligations of my job—all while making the crucial time for our new marriage and family. The daily demands of juggling the various facets of our lives were sometimes overwhelming. At times, it actually seemed impossible to do it all well. These were the years that I had to desperately pursue the Lord and put on my big girl panties.

I wanted more to life in my role of wife and mother than to dwell in emptiness and defeat. After unnecessary warring with my husband about what he wasn't doing or providing, I realized that I was shifting my reliance on my husband instead of onto my true Source. This in itself was not fair to him nor was it beneficial to our entire family.

Jesus than regained His rightful position as the center of my life. We live in a society that says that "You are every woman" and that as women we can multitask and handle a plethora of responsibilities all at one time. We are told we can balance a life of purpose in and outside of the home, fueling the myth of the superwoman. You are not alone nor do you have to put unneeded pressure on yourselves. Ladies, you have the ultimate King and Leader and the best Counselor and Concierge who will lead you into all truth and understanding. God, the Triune Being is the perfect combination for making you set for your childbearing experience and your impending role as a mother. You are not alone!

CHAPTER 2

SPIRITUAL CONCEPTION:

DEBUNKING THE CURSE

To the woman He said:
"I will greatly multiply your sorrow and your conception;
In pain you shall bring forth children;
Your desire shall be for your husband,
And he shall rule over you."
Genesis 3:16, NKJV

Many rely on the experience of generations of women before them to define their pregnancy and birth experience. It doesn't matter whether you are black, white, Hispanic, Asian, Jewish, Christian, or a combination of any of the above. Our culture has a set descriptive formula as to what pregnancy and childbirth should look like. You hear conversations strike up at the check-out line in the grocery store, at social gatherings among friends, or leisurely small talk at a child's play group that depict pregnancy and childbirth as being painful, a nuisance, burdensome, or intolerable.

These skewed notions are consistently reinforced by the images which are impressed on the minds of women who they see giving birth on television shows, in news stories, or written on websites. When my husband and I found out that we were pregnant with our son, Caleb, I thought to myself there has to be something different about my childbearing experience this time. The difference that I was thinking of did not come from the fact that he would not be a child born out of wedlock. If my life was to oppose the flesh, I didn't think that pregnancy and childbirth were to be the exception. The conviction that I had about birthing my children naturally became even stronger. I wanted to know what the Bible had to say about childbirth. I was in expectation that there would be a distinction from my pregnancy and childbirth in comparison to my first pregnancy with my daughter.

For decades Genesis 3:16 has been the Christian's blueprint and ultimate validation of the way a woman was destined to endure pregnancy and labor. Pastors, teachers, mothers, friends, and others have focused on a portion of Genesis 3:16 and many have overlooked the premise of God's judgment on Eve. Yes, God's instruction to Adam and Eve was not to eat of the tree of knowledge of good and evil. Yet, God's expectation was more prohibiting the first man and woman from eating that forbidden fruit. From day one, God was after our hearts. He wanted us to rely on Him for everything. However, in order to do His work on the earth, He created us in His image. Thus, He wired us so that His power was transmitted to our mind and through our mouths so that His words are spoken forth. After all, it was God's words that formed heaven and earth.

So, it is no surprise that the enemy is always attacking our minds. He knows that if he can get a hold of our minds, then he has an open door to our thoughts that leads to our heart which ultimately dictates our words and actions. So even though God gave Adam and Eve freedom and dominion, he restricted them from the tree of good and evil because he knew that the weight of the world would be too much for them to handle.

Parents know their children's strengths and weaknesses. During the early years of life, a parent teaches and guides their children because they know that too much freedom is counterproductive to their lives. I wouldn't give my three-year-old son the liberty of eating whatever he wants each day because I know that he would choose whatever his heart desires. I also wouldn't allow my eleven-year-old daughter the right to choose her bedtime because she would use that freedom to her detriment. Similarly, God created boundaries for Adam and Eve so that they would be redirected to Him.

Eve knew the instructions that God gave to her and to Adam. However, she allowed herself to entertain the deceitful words of the enemy. This ultimately caused her to consider a thought to be of more value than God's. She questioned and rationalized God's authority and role in their lives. She also allowed herself to shift her focus off of her purpose and to become distracted by something that was God's design, but was forbidden to them. Discontentment rose up in her heart as she focused on what she thought was more beneficial to her. The enemy used his eloquent words to entice her to think that she not only wanted the fruit but it was necessary for both she and her husband to survive.

It is amazing how these two so quickly took their purpose for granted, as though it was not valuable to God. In sum, Eve allowed her feelings to move her out of the will of God. This ultimately left her family vulnerable to destruction. Sin is contradictory to the will of God. Thus, it is the objective of the enemy to deceive us and try to separate us from the purpose and the plan that God has for our lives. God's instruction to

Adam and Eve was very clear; but the enemy was very manipulative as he twisted God's words.

Suddenly what was deemed a fact and the truth then became questionable and up for debate. Eve's mistake was that she did not shut down the conniving serpent; she continued to entertain and hold onto his cunning words. The second thought opened up doubt, discontentment, pride and arrogance in their hearts. The enemy didn't have to talk her ear off too long to get her to get on the path to disobedience.

Did someone or something ever distract you from your plans? It could be something as small as your desire to change your eating habits to something as extreme as relocating to another state or another country. The minute someone challenges the idea that you were committed to, you allow yourself to get distracted. Eve allowed herself to compare and discredit their portion as if she knew best. The fruit now looked more desirable because her heart became hardened to the truth.

I can see her having a whole conversation with herself as to how eating the fruit wasn't that big a deal. Eve was so lured into that deception that she even convinced herself that eating the fruit was not really that harmful to them. As we know, Eve was tempted by the serpent and both she and Adam ate the forbidden fruit.

Sin yields condemnation. She and Adam were consumed with fear after they disobeyed God's instructions. Prior to that Adam and Eve were in a state of bliss because they relied solely on God for their physical and spiritual needs. They knew that God would provide their every need when they were faithful to the assignment that He gave them. They indeed lacked no good thing. However, fear overwhelmed them when they questioned and looked to someone else's word as being higher than God's Word.

Since they allowed fear to rule them, it made it very hard for them to continue the assignment that God gave to them. They were distracted by fear. The thought of their wrongdoing sent them into a frenzy.

They assumed that their works were tied to God's love for them. Adam and Eve got busy trying to fix the problem they created, which led them to try being self-sufficient. But they allowed fear to separate them from the love of God. Fear paralyzed them even to the point of avoiding repentance.

Running from the sin that they committed seemed more logical than running to the One who could free them from the bondage that was created by the sin they committed.

Their communication with God was hindered by the fear that was now attached to them. Instead of running to God, they ran away from Him and thought that avoidance and passing the blame would give them resolution. As a parent, when I instruct my children to do something, I am enforcing instruction not for my own benefit, but for their protection. If they do not adhere to my instruction, then they are aware or will certainly learn that there are consequences for their actions.

Parents are given the responsibility to love their children in many ways. Discipline is one method. When a parent disciplines, the purpose is for the child to learn from a mistake but also so that they can realign themselves with their parent's authority. God was disciplining Eve and Adam for the sin they both had committed. So what was Eve's punishment? Pain during childbearing. However, the pain that God is referencing is not a physical pain.

Genesis 3:16, in several translations, correlates pain with sorrow. Pain is defined in Webster's dictionary as "a physical suffering." However, it is also defined as severe mental or emotional distress or suffering. Therefore, in proper context, God's penalty for women was not a physical pain, but an emotional pain.

The world was formed through words: God's words. Words were used for creative construction. However, when the serpent entered the garden, words were used for life-altering destruction. The enemy's tactic and goal was to destroy what was made for good. He succeeded when Adam and Eve took the bait and went against God's words. God gave both Adam and Eve the opportunity to redeem themselves by speaking the truth. However, they opted for self-preservation by using their words to destroy one another in attempts to dodge God's wrath. In a moment where they could have regained strength and integrity, Adam and Eve chose once again not to pursue and maintain righteousness. God's judgment was based on the terms that Adam and Eve chose—a commitment to living in fear.

The curse on man was not only a direct punishment against Adam and Eve; but on all future generations after them. Romans 5:12 speaks of all the generations following

Adam that would be of a sin nature; thus, spiritual death would follow. So woman would be subjected to dwell and grieve for her child being born into sin. God's sentence to multiply woman's grief explains the tendency for the mind of a mother, without warning, to be consumed with worry, doubt, frustration, and fear of the details pertaining to their child's life.

As a consequence, the ultimate purpose of the fall of man was to bring the woman back into submission and repentance for her actions. As the Father, God's goal was to correct the mind. This is where the power of the curse became a consequence for woman from conception to birth. According to Galatians 3:13, Christ redeemed us from the curse of the law. Therefore, that offers the liberty to anyone who accepts Jesus Christ as Lord and Savior to be saved by grace because of the ultimate sacrifice Jesus made.

Many have been taught that as a Believer, one inherits the blessing of Abraham, which guarantees success in a tangible form. However, the reason we can fully receive the blessing of Abraham is because of the decision to believe in God. Abraham's belief gave him the right to receive righteousness.

Our understanding of redemption from the curse of the law was given after the covenant was cut with Abraham. Since we our Abraham's seed, we have the same opportunity to be saved by grace through faith and be afforded righteousness as well. We are redeemed from the curse of the law which includes the fall of man, the covenant made with Abraham, and the law that was given to Moses for the Jewish people.

Romans 8:20-23 speaks to the grief and sorrow that generations following Adam and Eve had to endure because of their disobedience in the Garden. However, the Word goes on to confirm the confidence that we have in being redeemed through Christ Jesus. This allows us to have confidence through Jesus Christ in every area of our life, including conception, pregnancy, childbirth and motherhood. Our decision to believe in Jesus Christ results in a spiritual change. However as a result of our spiritual change, our physical needs are also changed.

Genesis 3:16 in its proper context shows that the curse on woman was a spiritual punishment causing her to experience grief because an innocent soul would be born into a world full of sin. Consequently, there is a spiritual war for the soul of the child. The Greek word for "pain" is *lupé*. The definition means pain of body or mind, grief or sorrow, as in the English translation. To understand pain contextually, what Eve would endure would be the pain, emotional grief and sorrow, multiplied in each stage of childbearing. For those who are attempting to conceive, there is the possibility of being grieved by the inability to conceive or the experience of an untimely conception.

The pregnant woman is overwhelmed with the increase of hormones and general concern for her pregnancy. The birthing mother is subjected to an increase of pain in childbirth because of being subjected to fear. Finally, motherhood can bring on distress and fear for a child's overall life and what a child can be exposed to in our sin-filled world. However, as believers, we hold to our faith in Jesus. We understand that our children are brought into a world of darkness. Nevertheless, we understand that God has a plan our children's lives. Thus, our mandate is to bring them up in reverence and admonition of the Lord.

It is also our responsibility to fix our minds to imitate the thoughts of Christ. It is only then that God becomes the true focus throughout the childbearing process because our foundation is firmly rooted. After our faith is anchored, we receive joy in what we know will feed our faith. And it is only then that our joy overcomes any fear. This is a monumental understanding especially concerning childbirth.

There is a direct connection to how fear impacts your body's response to pain in the birthing process. Our faith in Jesus overcomes any curse which allows us to rest in peace knowing that there is protection, healing, and just an overall covering for us as parents and our children.

CHAPTER 3

SPIRITUAL CHILDBEARING:

MAINTAINING YOUR PEACE

DURING PREGNANCY

AND BIRTH

Above all else, guard your heart,
for everything you do flows from it.
Keep your mouth free of perversity;
keep corrupt talk far from your lips.
Let your eyes look straight ahead;
fix your gaze directly before you.
Give careful thought to the paths for your feet
And be steadfast in all your ways.
Do not turn to the right or the left;
keep your foot from evil.
Proverbs 4:23-27, NIV

You may ask what does my pregnancy and birthing of my child have to do with any of this? It isn't that deep. If you are having these thoughts, you are sadly mistaken. There is a spiritual foundation that you need to set going into motherhood. This starts with preparing and executing your trust in God through the entirety of your childbearing experience. Your inability to trust God through the totality of your childbearing experience will hamper the foundation of your journey into motherhood. Key words are preparation and execution. You don't just start trusting God when your child is born; you establish the practice before the child is even a thought, which requires ongoing preparation before then.

It is similar to your journey into marriage. You don't suddenly begin trusting God about your marriage after your wedding vows are exchanged. Those who seek to have a godly marriage start preparing during their singleness, courtship, and engagement season so that they have the necessary tools to navigate the unknown. They want to know what to expect, what potential obstacles to avoid, and how to be successful in general.

However, after you have gone to every conference and received all of the advice available, it is your reliance on God to endure the unique journey in marriage. Likewise, you can read all of the books in the world regarding fertility, pregnancy, and motherhood, but the ultimate manual is not going to be a physical blueprint, but a spiritual one. Your trust and dependence on God is what is going to determine your success along the way. Your body, medical professionals, relatives, and friends are subject to fail you. However, the true living God will not.

There are frequent circumstances that we encounter throughout our lives that will test our trust in God.

Childbearing is one of them, and it is absolutely not the exception. Hebrews 11:1 (ESV), reads "…faith is the assurance of things hoped for, the conviction of things not seen." If childbearing is not one of the greatest examples of the need to employ faith, I don't know what is. But ultimately, our children are precious jewels that are gifts given to us. There is only one True Being who created us and is in charge of our lives— the true and Holy Living God. We cannot be so arrogant as to ever forget or allow anything to replace Him. Whether or not you plan a pregnancy, God was the One who saw fit to open your womb. He created that precious gift with all the intricate details for His own purpose. So, it is only fitting that you trust Him with the details of all of your child's life.

I understand that it is your child. *Believe* me, I do. I can recall with my first son, the doctors wanted to monitor his brain development. During my first sonogram at 21 weeks, a cyst was detected growing on his brain. Now, the doctors were not concerned because they said that it was common and usually it would go away and would not be a cause for concern. However, they wanted to be on the safe side and schedule a second sonogram at 34 weeks. The following three months, I could have cried my eyes out every day. I could have talked to a multitude of friends and family about the situation. My every thought could have been consumed with the matter. I chose to rely on God to continue completing this wonderfully made boy. I chose to meditate on what was good concerning my pregnancy.

And at the second ultrasound, the technicians and doctors reported that the cyst was no longer there. I choose to think of childbearing as a preliminary test for motherhood. You think that childbearing is a huge undertaking? Then what will you do when doctors diagnose your child with a disability or what if your child wants to start associating with a group of children that are not God's best for them or what if your child begins to question his belief in God. That is when we can discuss what it means to endure pain.

It is going to take complete trust in God throughout the entirety of your child's life. We know that life begins at conception. The time to decide to trust God is from the moment you see that positive symbol on the pregnancy stick. As we know for ourselves, life does not get any easier as we get older. The trials get harder, sometimes longer, and more complex. As mothers, and more importantly regarding our children, we cannot afford to allow ourselves to take on that care. Our families are relying on our presence to set the atmosphere in the home. As wives and mothers, we play such a pivotal role in ensuring that the home and family are taken care of.

When I was first pregnant with my daughter, I thought that I would succeed if I mirrored my experience with a woman whom I highly valued and looked to her having all of the answers to navigate life—none other than my mother. She was and is still in my opinion, one of the greatest women I've known. My mother is the epitome of having a servant's heart. She is so caring, giving, nurturing, and exudes strength.

I was 21 years old and pregnant with no experience of raising a child. Yes, I had experience with assisting parents with their children for a few hours here and there. But a part-time job is nothing in comparison to training up the next generation on a full-time basis. While I was naturally gifted in taking care of children, I was now given the ultimate responsibility of raising my own and as a single mother at that. Albeit support came after her birth, I was consumed with my thoughts of how I would continue college, work, and raise my daughter. By His grace, God wired me with endurance and perseverance. So, I just did what I knew to do which was to continue to take one step at a time; failure was not an option now.

Nonetheless, failure occurred in other forms during my first pregnancy. Like many women, no matter the age, I overindulged for all of the wrong reasons. I became an emotional eater. If I was depressed, I would entertain any craving to make my emotional pain go away. Many would validate my need to fulfill my craving and I, too, would buy into the inaccurate idea of "eating for two" or that the "baby wanted it." I had no self-control at all.

It could be 10:00 at night and if I had a craving for cheesecake, I would travel miles searching until I found a place to buy it. The next day, my mind would then be fixed to think that I needed it. And you better believe I would go right back to fulfilling my craving because I had allowed myself to think that I needed it or better yet the baby "wanted it."

I specifically remember having a cheeseburger with fries from a local diner after each one of my childbirth and baby care classes. It became a part of the after class routine. It didn't matter how much my doctor had advised me to reduce my calorie intake. In my mind, I deserved it since I was juggling a full load of courses at school while also working full-time. Anytime I felt lonely and unsure of my future or my daughter's future, my mind would go into autopilot and search for something sweet or salty. Or anytime, I felt like I "needed" to feed a craving," I gave in.

Self-control was not any stronger for me back then. I knew that having a healthy baby would include having a natural birth, without medication and breastfeeding my baby thereafter. But I did not have the mental fortitude to complete my goal of a natural and healthy birth. My emotions and thoughts were a conundrum of ups and downs. I equated childbirth, like most women, to an extraordinary amount of pain. I supported my belief with the dramatic scenes of a woman panting frantically or wailing. I watched shows like this religiously because I wanted to be prepared for childbirth.

Many ask me about the key to having a successful pregnancy and childbirth. My answer has never wavered; the key to each stage is renewing your mind to focus on peace. In God's presence, there is righteousness and peace. If you do not decide to be intentional about staying in His Word and in His presence daily, you will encounter difficulty handling the physical and spiritual pressures. When you make the decision to live a life of seeking daily bread, you will establish God's peace to rule your heart and mind. You cannot expect to be at peace when you are not guarding your heart and mind at all times, especially when people are so willing to speak fear into your life.

"Life and death are in the power of the tongue; and they should eat of the fruit thereafter" (Proverbs 18:21). Our words that we speak come from a series of thoughts that we meditate on, which stems from our heart. But if we keep our minds set on Jesus, we will remain in perfect peace because of our trust in Him (Isaiah 26:3). In addition, it is all the more important to identify when the enemy is trying to attack your mind.

The enemy will try and use every tactic to get you to discredit God's Word. It is so important to be aware of the devourer and how he tries to sneak into our lives. You know he is always going to use the "backdoor" through our minds. He is ultimately after our peace. He is going to always get us to question God's Word through doubt, worry, covetousness, pride, and selfishness.

This is why it is so important to make sure that you are guarding your heart and mind. If you let down your guard, you are subject to let your flesh be moved by the negative stories or suggestions about your pregnancy or you will entertain and act on any plan that your medical professionals or family members instruct you to do.

It is so important that we do not make decisions that are based in fear. Our decisions that we make during our pregnancy can have a major impact on childbirth, and sometimes as far as our child's overall well being. Thus, you have to be very selective about who you choose to speak into your life. Conversations have the ability to influence your opinion on particular topics. It will make all the difference in the world to have mature and strong women to keep you accountable. However, it is just as important that you do not allow their thoughts, opinions, and life become your only source.

I was also spiritually malnourished. This is why it is so important to understand the Word for yourself and to gain understanding. Mothers play an important role in the family. We guard and watch over our household and this requires that we become well-informed and seek out wisdom. So when I read an article, listen to a message, or take into account a professional's diagnosis, I ask myself 'Who said...? or 'Does this line up with what I am believing for or better yet does it align with the Word of God?' I would often ask people 'Who said?' or 'How are you coming to that conclusion?' I would often challenge people about their source of information.

I remember like it was yesterday. A woman at church came up to me and asked 'Are you afraid about going into labor?' I know that she didn't mean any harm. However in an effort to guard against fear entering my mind, I kindly asked, 'Who said I should be afraid of labor? I am trusting God in all the matters of my pregnancy and labor. I will not entertain fear or worry.' You have to be vigilant and relentless in ensuring that the right things are entering your eyes, ears, and mind.

The life of a Christian includes experiencing spiritual warfare. It does not stop at pregnancy, labor and delivery. "Do not be anxious about anything, but in everything, by prayer and petition, with thanksgiving, present your requests to God. And the peace of God, which transcends all understanding, will guard your hearts and your minds in Christ Jesus" (Philippians 4:6-8). Ladies, we have to encourage each other in every season, including pregnancy, labor, and delivery. No one is going to give you a medal for having a quick and painless delivery. However, they sure are not going to give you an award for the longest and most traumatized experience either! The best support anyone can give a pregnant woman is love and encouragement.

Now in regards to the suggestions and advice of people, be selective about who speaks into your life. I have a small, select number of friends that I allow to speak into my life and give advice. However, even with those friends, I still do my part, which includes researching for a reliable opinion. As far as taking orders, getting information and advice from doctors, please let me be clear, that I am certainly not going to be super religious and tell you to disregard sound wisdom that is given by doctors. With each of my pregnancies, I have and continue to believe in a healthy and natural pregnancy, labor and delivery. If my practitioners had a concern or gave me some advice or instructions I would always take what they shared into consideration and then accept or reject after researching to my satisfaction.

God forbid if I were in a life or death situation where a decision had to be made quickly on my health and the health of my child, the baby would always come before my hopes and desires. However, my decisions are made based on the peace that I have after I pray about the matter. You also have every right to get a second professional opinion, if necessary. This is why selecting your doctor, practice, hospital, or birthing center with care and discernment is so important. You have to ensure that their beliefs and practices align with what you want your experience to be.

Our society has been driven to rely on technology for everything—to maintain relationships, employment, education, and to some their health. People and information is available at the snap of a finger. Although the internet, social media, and apps have worked to our advantage, it has also been our downfall as well. Some people have made these resources and the people behind technology like gods. We've all been there, I know I have. You come across a minor issue and we run straight to Google.

Social media has been another platform that society has used to find comfort and answers. Don't get me wrong, social media is a great tool when used correctly. However, we have to make sure that it and the people using it, are put in the proper perspective. A harmless post can plant seeds of worry, fear, and contention in your mind in a matter of seconds.

For example, I often see people post questions to seek advice regarding a pregnancy symptom that they are experiencing. And without a second thought, they are guaranteed to hear from that one person who will share their own personal horror story, which adds no value to the innocent inquiry. The next thing you know, a chorus of women will chime in with their traumatic stories as if each experience would trump the other. Or better yet, you post a picture of yourself at a baby care class and someone will comment off topic regarding their horrible experience in labor or postpartum. You can be inundated with an overload of opinions.

It may seem harmless to you as though their opinion does not matter. However, whether you believe it or not, each comment is a seed that was sown. The more seeds of the same fruit that are sown, the greater the ability they have to influence your thoughts and actions; especially if you are not replacing the negativity with what the Word of God says. Temptation can test your ability to utilize self-control and discipline. It is wise to know your limitations. However, God knows that we are not perfect beings and that the flesh is weakened by the sin nature. Use social media wisely.

Conversations that are filled with what everyone thinks about your questions, thoughts, or feelings can distract you from your goals. It is best to evaluate the words that you speak or the conversation that we entertain whether or not it will have any benefit to our life. Many, especially friends and family, can all be coming from a good place and have the best of intentions. Nevertheless, we have to be intentional to fix our thoughts on the Word of God.

There is purpose behind the instruction and plans that God has for us. It is through our trust that we gain security in knowing that through it all, He will not fail us. After Adam and Eve ate of the tree of good and evil, they reacted with the "flight or fight" defense mechanism. They did not want to take ownership for their actions. Fear motivated them to think of how they could rectify their disobedience in their strength. Fear had a great impact on their thought process. When God gave them the opportunity to do what was right, they began to play the blame game.

Self-control is an area that has to be developed. We will not be able to see any fruit of this discipline with others, if it is not a discipline in our minds. It takes control to not always have a masterful comeback for the person who speaks ill of you. How do you think you are going to have enough self-control during labor if you are not able to control your will to turn down a French fry? Better yet, how are you going to have a sweet and loving tone with your toddler when he is a having a terrific tantrum when you do not have the same patience towards your husband who didn't follow through with your request to take out the trash? You cannot continue to play the blame game because of the up and down hormones.

The increasing and fluctuating hormones during pregnancy are real! Yes, everyone's experience varies but we have still been given the same opportunity to decide to control our emotions. As a Christians, our standard is not to allow ourselves to be emotionally led throughout the day. We have the same responsibility to die to our flesh, whether we are pregnant or not. There is no "Stay in Your Emotions Pass" when you're pregnant. God did not say "You should be holy, for I am holy" (1 Peter 1:16) except for when you're pregnant. Don't you know that God knows and understands the demands of your mind and body? This is all the more reason to yield to the Holy Spirit throughout your day. He is looking for you to depend on Him every day to take on what you cannot handle in your own strength. We all have been charged to operate under the same grace of the Holy God.

The Bible does not speak of a guarantee to have a carefree and symptom-free childbearing experience when you are living a righteous life. It is imperative that as Christians we employ our faith in every area of our lives. However, we have to ensure that we are lining up our lives through the living Word of God; and not use fantasy or take scriptures out of context to fit our own agendas.

For example, I have heard some try to use scripture to support their belief that Christian women have the right to have a quick and painless childbirth. In my opinion, it is a real stretch to use the word in Exodus that midwives reported back to Pharaoh about the Hebrew women giving birth quickly. If you read in context, Pharaoh instructed the midwives to kill all of the male babies. But the midwives referenced and feared God so their account to Pharaoh was purposely misleading in an effort to save the lives of the babies, including their own. In 1 Timothy 2:15, the scripture does speak to how women can be saved through childbearing: "continue in faith, love, and holiness with self-control."

It is our duty to have complete trust in God through the entirety of our pregnancy into motherhood. Our inability to maintain a life that is consecrated to God is our inability to serve our family and ultimately live a life of worship to Him. The Apostle Paul in 2 Timothy 2:15 validates our childbearing experience being determined by our spiritual fruits. During pregnancy, there are so many symptoms that may occur along the way. You may say how can I keep my peace when I am either emotionally drained or physically in pain. The Lord will keep you in perfect peace, but you have to decide to keep your mind fixed on Him. When we get our focus off of the symptom, the fear, the problem, needing the solution, and onto God who provides healing and strength when we are weak, we enter into a place of contentment.

Philippians 4:11-13 states, "Not that I am speaking of being in need, for I have learned in whatever situation I am to be content. I know how to be brought low, and I know how to abound. In any and every circumstance, I have learned the secret of facing plenty and hunger, abundance and need. I can do all things through him who strengthens me." When we allow each day to be one of intentional worship for the true King of Kings, He provides a way that does not come from within. Our job to simply do what the Apostle Paul was speaking of: "continue in faith, love, and holiness with self-control."

CHAPTER 4

SPIRIT FOOD FOR THE SINGLE,

PREGNANT MOTHER:

MAINTAINING A SPIRITUAL DIET

& OVERCOMING CONDEMNATION

By this we shall know that we are of the truth and
reassure our heart before him;
for whenever our heart condemns us,
God is greater than our heart, and he
knows everything. Beloved, if our heart does not condemn us,
we have confidence before God;

1 John 3:19-21, ESV

It was a few days before Christmas 2002, while everyone was finishing up their shopping and going to Christmas parties, I was contemplating whether or not to announce my pregnancy to my daughter's father and my parents. There was never any doubt in my mind whether I was going to continue my pregnancy or not. This was not my first pregnancy; I had terminated my pregnancy with my first child two years prior. Due to my low self-esteem, I was in an unhealthy repetitive cycle of going from one relationship to the next. If it seemed right, I bought into the game that led into nothing more than giving up my time, money, and more importantly my value and worth. Every time, I allowed myself to be a young woman of his convenience in the bedroom. There were no long walks, definitely no intimate and lengthy conversation. While I was searching for love and acceptance, he was searching for the quickest way he could get me in bed. And even when a man would attempt to start the relationship the right way, I cheapened it with sex because I was naïve enough to believe it was the way to initiate and keep love.

When I found out that I was pregnant the first time, I was so scared and did not know what to do. I was a first semester freshman in college. I was in a long distance relationship with my high school sweetheart at the time. Since I did not understand the purpose of love, I did not honor it. Thus I cheapened the relationship I was in, by finding someone to fill the physical absence of someone who genuinely loved me. I knew that the pregnancy would be a disappointment to so many. Therefore, fear led me to make the decision to abort the pregnancy. There was so much guilt and many unhealed wounds from the trauma that the abortion caused. I had such a great love for children. This made it ten times more distressing to come to cope with ending my child's life.

Hurt on top of loneliness would seep into my heart leading me to a persistent battle with depression. This was one of the loneliest times in my life because I felt like no one understood my perspective at the time. I promised myself that if I was ever in a predicament like that again, that I wouldn't make a decision that was based out of fear, outside pressure, or what I thought people wanted me to do. I never would have thought that I would be in the same position and so soon. However, I was far from living a life consecrated to God. Thus my mind was not renewed; so it was an open invitation to be led down the same path again. I knew that getting pregnant, for the second time at that, outside of marriage was not God's best for me. Nevertheless, I knew that having another abortion wasn't either. So, I pushed forward without looking back or entertaining any additional conversation with anyone.

I received so much static from my choice in continuing my pregnancy. This was one of my man run-ins with fighting people bondage. I knew that everyone was going to have an opinion and that they did. I had everyone from my boss giving subtle threats as to what could happen if I continued my pregnancy to girls at my college asking me how I could have gotten into the "predicament." However, this was the moment where I had at least an ounce of the fear of God in me. The other part of me was determined to have a second chance. In my mind it was a second time of redemption. However, it wasn't until later that I would understand how I could redeem my life. I knew that there was a great possibility that I would be going through parenthood alone. I was just willing to take my chances this time around.

So, I just continued to put one foot in front of the other each day. Each day; I continued my regular routine to wake up and go to bed each day in my dormitory room, go to class and from there go to work. The stares and the whispers continued but what rang louder were the lies the enemy would tell me that I couldn't manage the load, that I wouldn't be able to raise and provide for my daughter, that the continued pressure would be too much. Yet, I pushed forward but in ways that were not necessarily beneficial to me overall – emotionally eating. There was no open exchange towards accountability because I had built up a wall to reject anyone that seemed like they were coming against me and not being supportive emotionally or mentally. My heart could not take any more rejection.

Condemnation is the battle that weighs heavily in many people's minds – especially single mothers. There is harsh direct or indirect judgment and disapproval from many. Although the church teaches to reject condemnation, in the same vein it has the potential to seep through some of the pulpits to parishioners and leaders towards others. I had grown up in church and had seen the stares of ushers criticizing the style of a young lady's dress or whispers of a member's disapproval of a child's behavior and what the parents were or were not doing to their satisfaction.

At a church that I attended, members were even asked to consider standing before the congregation to ask for forgiveness for whatever sin they had committed. Typically it was a sin where the consequence was visible. I recalled seeing the shame on their faces and their heads hung low. It wasn't even embarrassment that I felt for them, it was more so sympathy. I would see and hear these youth and sometimes adults occasionally give an account of their sin and ask for forgiveness. As I got older, I would think to myself how wrong and unjust to ask someone to consider this public display just in God's eyes. I would later find myself in this predicament, which led me to leave the church. I was going to respectfully leave everything that I knew.

This was the end of my chapter at that place of worship. However, the circumstance did not draw me closer to Christ; neither did it push me to seek truth and understanding. My heart and my absence later drew me further away from the church and hardened my heart. I still sought out going to another church but it left me finding religion as opposed to seeking a relationship with Christ. I knew that I should go to church; but my inward battle with gaining knowledge, left me achieving the bare minimum by just attending church. There was no pursuit of gaining a personal relationship with the Lord. I had so many imperfections and the church that I had come from made you feel that you were only worth something through your performance. I knew that my "performance" in life was far from excellent.

I walked around empty and void. I didn't purposefully pursue a relationship with Jesus because in my head I didn't have it all together and that I wouldn't be accepted in my broken state. In my mind, I wouldn't be able to gain a relationship with the Lord until I was older and had "it together."

Condemnation is the breeding ground for a life in bondage to people. A person who does not accept the freedom of their life in Christ accepts a life sentence to people bondage. They navigate through life allowing someone else's words to weigh in heavier than what they themselves believe or more importantly what God says. This is a scary and deadly place to be in. You cannot serve two masters; and when you decide to allow other people's words to weigh in heavier than God's words you are heading down a road to destruction. People bondage would personally continue to rear its ugly head because I was so consumed with what other people had to say or did not say about my life. This had been something that I didn't just deal with as an adult but could not shake when I was younger. My self-esteem was always super low. I didn't value my inward or outward worth because I felt rejected by my peers and even by some of my family members.

Although I came from a two-parent household, my father was silent for many years of my life because he was always busy outside of the home focused on his corporate job. When he was home, he did not engage me or cover me spiritually. While he was busy trying to financially and materially provide the best life possible for me, I was looking for his approval. I did not receive the validation because his words did not always match his intent. Like most parents, he did the best that he knew how to do in the moment. However, I later learned how his actions and my failure to let go, forgive, and heal would have an impact on my present and future relationships. While people in my family and circle of friends would attempt to build me up, I would constantly reject their words because their words didn't match up with what I perceived the "majority" to think of me.

I attended school in predominately white districts all my life. The teachers and students embraced me and loved me for the most part. However, my physical differences each passing year became more apparent to the point I didn't feel comfortable in my own skin. Commentary about my hair being "poofy," or questions about me wearing braids, or not being thin enough or tall enough started to eat away at my confidence. My lack of confidence not only affected my personal relationships at times but my performance in school.

I never wanted class attention on me because of my inability to read without fumbling my words when I read out loud or my tendency to break into sweats or turning red when required to present in front of the class. There were often times that I would have a mild case of stuttering because I was so nervous when I was in the spotlight. Although I appreciated those who supported me, I always wanted to be loved by those who I believe did not support me. I always wanted to be accepted. I wanted to be a part of everyone's life. If I got the impression that someone did not approve of something I did or said, I would work hard to try to gain their approval. It did not matter, if it inconvenienced me or if it was not for my benefit. I had to make things right all the time.

Since I continued to value people's opinions of me into adulthood, I had to navigate the stares and whispers when I was pregnant with my daughter. I tried to adapt to whatever scenario or circumstance I was placed in. So I always made sure that I carried myself modestly and avoided wearing t-shirts and jeans. I always attempted to make sure I didn't draw attention to the empty ring finger on my left hand. As I didn't want to give people the opportunity to confirm my single status. I would always hide behind my eloquent words and whatever education or degrees that I had obtained to confirm that I was the exception to rule of statistics. Nevertheless, I was not able to draw attention away from my young face and baby bump, or later on the baby, which could not allow me to retreat from the ultimate stigma that I wanted to avoid: young, single mother.

I knew my new role as a mother would come with responsibilities that were greater than myself. The weight of the decisions that I would have to make concerning another person was not a light matter. My child's life was going to mirror the opportunities that I made available to her. It was going to be important to me that I invest in the quality of her life by drawing attention to her education and shaping her world by being exposed to different opportunities. It was only a matter of time before I would come to the understanding that my limited view was not the prime focus of being a mother and raising a child. My life and ultimately the life of my child was going to be much bigger than both us.

Although I was tested and tried throughout my life into motherhood, I renounced the strong hold that people's opinion had on my life when I had an encounter with Jesus. It was 2007 and I was struggling to break free from my soul tie with my daughter's father. It was only then that the blinders were taken off of so many broken places in my life. I knew in that moment in August 2007 that I would truly have a heart of repentance and rededicate my life to Christ.

There were no more playing games or pity parties or allowing temptation to woo me anymore. I had to regain my integrity and more than anything my right standing and fellowship with God. It wasn't until I had my daughter that I was determined to challenge myself to be the example that I knew she needed but that I needed for myself. I understood that this would only be accomplished by making intentional decisions to stop hanging with the same friends since I knew that they were not going to point me back to Christ. I also knew that my life of going to the club and breaking myself slowly but surely from the music and television shows that I watched and replacing it with new hobbies, hangouts, and music that would not allow my emotions or thinking to saying or doing anything that was counterintuitive with my reestablished walk with Christ. Ultimately, I would need to renew my mind so that I could start having new thoughts that were in line with the Word of God. Eliminating bad habits without replacing them with new habits is just as ineffective to keeping them.

Once I found a church home and godly friends to hold me accountable, I was able to further strengthen my walk with the Lord. But the work had to start with my personal relationship with Him. It was during my new walk that He started slowly healing me of some deeps wounds.

The first item on the agenda was taking off my old nature and getting free from condemnation. I was still holding onto all of the past mistakes, past rejections, past abortions and all of the emotions that came with the baggage. I had to renounce my thinking that I could "do it all by myself." "I'm a boss," "Who runs the world" mentality and realign myself with the Lord. It was only then that I was fully able to surrender my life knowing and receiving the covering, provision and protection that only He would be able to perfect in any situation that my child and I would encounter.

There was something so freeing about yielding myself to Him. I slowly came to an understanding and received peace that I didn't have to know all the answers; neither did I have put on display that I was perfect with no issues. It was time after time after time that as I continued to trust God that He would provide answers and eliminate anything that was not of Him. In His presence I was freed from the opinions of others because I knew that regardless of what I saw, how I felt, or who was coming against me that He would make it work out for our good.

Romans 8:1, 5-6 says: "There is therefore now no condemnation for those who are in Christ Jesus. For those who live according to the flesh set their minds on the things of the flesh, but those who live according to the Spirit set their minds on the things of the Spirit. For to set the mind on the flesh is death, but to set the mind on the Spirit is life and peace."

Sister, life will never be perfect. Yes, there is going to be a whole bunch of questions left unanswered; there are going to be times that you will feel like giving up; there are going to be times that you question what you got yourself into. But I can guarantee you one thing, the best decision right after saying yes to your baby's life, is giving all your rights and wrongs

77

along with your baby's entire life back to the Lord. You cannot focus on your past. There is still so much in store. You ask how God can turn it around. I would ask myself this question constantly early on and then I was reminded of 1 Corinthians 1:26-31: "For consider your calling, brothers: not many of you were wise according to worldly standards,[a] not many were powerful, not many were of noble birth. But God chose what is foolish in the world to shame the wise; God chose what is weak in the world to shame the strong; God chose what is low and despised in the world, even things that are not, to bring to nothing things that are, so that no human being[b] might boast in the presence of God. And because of him[c] you are in Christ Jesus, who became to us wisdom from God, righteousness and sanctification and redemption, so that, as it is written, "Let the one who boasts, boast in the Lord."

There is no manual for motherhood; and I can promise you that there is no master plan to raising a child in a single parent household either. But God, He makes things all new and He has the ultimate plan for you and your child's life. He knew of your baby's existence before you saw the positive sign on the pregnancy stick. There is a purpose and plan for you and your child's life. It is time to stop looking to your baby's father, your parents, your friends, your favorite celebrity for all the answers. God is all you need and He will complete the good work that He started in both of you.

CHAPTER 5

LEADING MOM INTO PEACE:

HUSBAND AND BIRTH SUPPORT

ADVOCATE IN CHILDBEARING

My Husband's Perspective:

From the beginning of time when God made man in His image and after His likeness, a responsibility or ability to respond has been given to men to be the spiritual, emotional, and physical leader, protector, and provider. We have been given this awesome mandate by which God has entrusted lives into our hands. That alone is a great task that should be joyful, yet it can be overwhelming. I know it was and still is for me.

As I was inspired to write, you will find that I will refer back to the full duty of a husband in a household since the standards are equally important while caring for a wife throughout her pregnancy and into birth of the child. I pray that this will be insightful information that will be of use to prospective fathers. As you can see, my wife is very passionate about the life cycle from pregnancy to child rearing. As her husband, I take interest in her passions to ensure that I continue in the role as her covering.

As a husband, you are the leader of your household and make no mistake about it. However, this is not a position to be domineering by any means, but rather to lead in love and to exemplify what Ephesians 5:25 states, "Husbands love your

81

wives, as Christ loved the church and gave himself up for her…" That simply means a man should love his wife in such a way that she has no other choice but to see him as the leader of the home and to see that his word does carry weight in her heart. This can only be accomplished through time spent showing action after action reassuring your wife that you care for her.

Whenever the subject of pregnancy comes up with men, the majority of the time the first words are "Man, I'm not ready to be a father!" or "I don't know if I can provide for a baby yet." And I get it. I felt the same way. It may have been for different reasons, but I understand that line of thinking. At the moment you and your wife find out that you are expecting, she is looking to you for affirmation of whether this is a joyous occasion or if this is added stress to your already busy life. Remember, you set the tone of how this pregnancy is going to go.

This is time when being the leader in the area of emotions becomes a huge factor. I know from experience because my wife and I had two unexpected pregnancies and both times it was when we were attempting to establish a solid family foundation from moving to a better place, paying off debt, or attempting to further our careers. However, those plans were put on hold by the arrival of our children.

Immediately, my wife looked to me for assurance that everything would be okay, and to be quite honest I failed at giving that emotional leadership that she needed at the time. That, for a time, set the tone for the pregnancy. Looking back our situation, because of how deeply our Leader and Provider God looks out for us His children daily, I had nothing to be stressed out about. You have to ensure that your wife understands that she will not be in this alone and to constantly affirm that your presence will be consistent throughout her pregnancy and beyond.

The most comforting thing to any woman is to see her husband active and attentive to needs in the birthing process, which will continue to validate your role as the leader in the home. It is important to understand that you have to guard your emotions at all times and be protective of your wife's emotions. At times this may seem difficult, but it is important to understand that Christ is empowering you to be able to properly lead your wife in this area because since you are her covering.

We automatically equate our role as being the provider and we think that role equates to making enough money. Though that is a part of our leadership, there is a bigger picture in that providing an environment in the home is essential to maintaining peace in the home. As a man, understand that you are to protect the peace of your home at all costs. I can't begin to tell you how draining it is to be in a home where the head of the home is constantly stressed out and worry captivates and controls the atmosphere. You can imagine the direct effect that has on your wife and unborn child. If money is the direct cause of the stress in the home, I strongly suggest you seek wisdom from God on getting provision another way.

There is no dollar amount that is worth the undue stress in a household. I know first hand about financial stress because with both of my wife's pregnancies I was unemployed. The first time I was let go with a severance package because my employer's site was closing down. The second time I was terminated two months before the entire site was shut down once again.

If you want to talk about an opportunity for elevated stress levels in the home, that was it. However, after spending time with God after the second termination while my wife was pregnant, I needed answers and that's when I knew that I needed to relocate my family to Atlanta. I came to understand that God was looking to relocate us sooner so he had to allow those jobs to dry up to get us to the place we should have been. So knowing where you should be and where you are taking your family plays a huge role in the provision that you give your family.

When the time comes for your wife to give birth, there are important leadership skills needed in this process as well. Typically a man may think that there is not much for him to do at this point; that the process is all between the doctor and your wife. However, in many aspects you are right, but you are still the leader, protector, provider even in the delivery room.

With our first pregnancy, I was at work when my wife went into labor. She texted me from home that morning saying that she was ready to deliver the baby. After she monitored her contractions, later that morning, she sent me another text asking me to come home because she was definitely in labor. And from there as I jumped in the car speeding down the highway to get home, I still had to keep my emotions in check so that when I reached home, I didn't tense up and stress her out. I made it home in record time and I began to get everything together.

My wife wanted to stay home a little longer. However, I knew I heard the Holy Spirit say it was time to go. I had to be confident enough to know even in the small things I hear from God for the protection of my wife, even if she wanted to disagree. So we arrived at the hospital and went straight to the maternity ward to be greeted by nurses who checked in my wife. Immediately, they state that we would be there for a long while. So after getting settled and approval, we went for a walk in the hallway.

A short while after, I hear again from the Holy Spirit directing me that we should return back to the room. So, I relay the instructions to my wife and no sooner than we return to the room, her water breaks after the nurse she examined her. She immediately called the medical team in and within minutes our son was born. God directed me throughout the entire time and in obedience I was able to lead my wife confidently. Many would say as a man you should shut up and sit down. You have no role to play. Your obedience matters even in the small things of your life. Had I not listened to the voice of the Holy Spirit we could have had our son at home, in the car, or in the hallway of the hospital. This reminds me of John 16:13 where the Holy Spirit comes to lead and guide in all truth.

Now with the birth of our youngest son, my wife was beginning to get a revelation of freedom from fear of birthing. So my role was different. We wanted a delivery in peace with the least amount of stress as possible. So instead of giving her instructions, my role was giving her affirmation and ensuring that my emotions were in check throughout the entire time so that we didn't fill the room with tension.

As my wife used the hypnobirthing method, which the nurse was unfamiliar with and the doctor stated that she had witness women "attempt" to use it--I had to be a great teammate by continuing to affirm my wife despite the pushback that we were receiving from the medical staff. In the moment as a husband, I still had to make sure to protect my wife from any negativity and advocate for her so that we stuck to our birth plan. By the end of the delivery by staying focus and doing it our way, the skeptical doctor and the apprehensive nurse were requesting that my wife come teach classes on hypnobirthing.

Imagine if I would have wavered and applied pressure to my wife to go with the medical professionals that would have been one less way to prove that birthing can be a fearless process. So that day we made a believer that God can make your pregnancy and delivery a fearless process and we don't have to feed into the social norm of what this process looks like. There is another way. I am reminded of 1 Corinthians 1:26-28 where it states that God chose what is considered insignificant and unpopular in this world to confound man's limited knowledge to show if we chose *His* way, His knowledge is always greater!

My Mother's Perspective:

"You know exactly how I was made, bit by bit, how I was sculpted from nothing into something.Like an open book, you watched me grow from conception to birth;all the stages of my life were spread out before you, The days of my life all prepared before I'd even lived one day." (Psalm 139, The Message)

How could anyone read those words and not believe that God thought of us even before our parents did? And regardless of who your parents are, you were first birthed in the womb of God's heart.

That fact is why I love pastor and prolific author, Rick Warren's declaration, that "there are no illegitimate children; though there may be illegitimate parents." Being born out of wedlock myself, I took great solace in those words.

One of my favorite roles on this side of eternity has been motherhood. So it thrills me that Nadra Dyan Cohens chose to write her first book about the experience of childbirth. When I first came face to face with the author more than three decades ago, I was clueless about who this person that God placed in my womb would become. (Yes, I'm her proud mom.) Now with all certainty, I see that God graced her with the ability to seek and find Him in all circumstances—the good, the bad, and the ugly. Only through her relationship with Him could she have been led to share with you about the first phase of this noble calling of motherhood.

It has been my privilege to be present at the birth of all three of my grandchildren and on the delivery of my granddaughter, I served as Nadra's birth coach. Each labor and delivery was quite different and not simply because of the length or intensity of the experience. With her I have experienced the body, the mind, and the spirit of childbirth. What I've seen is how the God-connection makes a remarkable difference. It's so much more than reproducing because you have the reproductive equipment.

The journey through the pregnancy, labor and delivery of Azaria Renee, was a time of uncertainty, anxiety, and even fear—for both of us. (Imagine your birth coach telling you you're not in labor.) From the beginning, I knew I could never be this baby's surrogate father, but for my daughter, I was willing to be the hand-holder, the encourager, the source of unconditional love that a woman needs in those emotional nine months. In her case, a young, single college co-ed, facing the unknown alone, only made pregnancy and childbirth more ominous. Despite her circumstance, she boldly said "yes" to her baby girl's life. It was a God-honoring choice. And for me, I concluded that Azaria's arrival was a fulfillment of Psalm 30:5—"weeping may endure for a night, but joy comes in the morning." She was born at 8:01 a.m.

When I was invited to join Nadra and her husband Channing for the delivery and birth of Caleb Bryant, I saw that eight years made a world of difference. It was more than taking the childbirth classes with her husband in a small, private setting instead of in a hospital. She used the techniques from the class and that was coupled with the truth of love casting out fear. It set an entirely different tone for Caleb's arrival. I did wonder if my son-in-law would survive Nadra's chokeholds when she clung to his neck with each contraction as they paced the labor ward corridor.

It was pregnancy number three when the beauty of childbirth unfolded. The childbirth education classes/hypnobirthing course she took while she was pregnant with Cayden Blair made a world of difference and took her to an entirely new level of preparing for delivery.

This time the picture was completely different: Her soundtrack was worship music filling her ear; her groans, as

Romans 8:26 says "too deep for words;" her gentle rolling on the exercise ball, all created the setting for her communion with God as he transferred her baby boy from His hands to hers.

I wrote in my journal, "She was amazing!" I'm not saying she didn't experience any pain or discomfort. In fact, there was a moment when she reminded me of what it must have been like for Peter when Jesus called him to walk to Him on water. She, like Peter, began to look at the waves (of contractions). For a moment, she took her eyes off Jesus, and began to panic and cry out. But Channing redirecting her during that crescendo of pain steadied her and before long, Cayden made his appearance. As she yielded to the Spirit, the Prince of Peace blanketed her. The only way I can describe the third birth is a spiritual encounter.

Not only was I awestruck, but the attending obstetrician, who periodically would offer pain medication, was amazed at Nadra turning down her offers. Not surprisingly an AMA-certified physician would dismiss something like hypnobirthing. But in this case, she asked Nadra to drop her business cards at her office; another confirmation that God was with my daughter in a new and fresh way.

Labor, delivery, and childbirth are different for every woman. Just as different as our fingerprints. I do pray her testimony will be a source of encouragement that brings you to the acknowledgment of Romans 8:28, "And we know that God causes all things to work together for good to those who love God, to those who are called according to His purpose."

Should you have the privilege of being involved as a birth coach or a support to a couple there are very helpful things that you can do on Labor Day and beyond.

Carry along a bag of goodies for both mom and dad. Water, juice, fruit, granola bars, nuts, and other snacks are a great addition to the usual gear of pillows, lip balm, cozy socks or nursing nightgowns. Dad will need to be encouraged as well as Mom. Sometimes you can communicate your approval with just a smile or a hug because there are moments when there are no appropriate words other than, "Jesus!"

If you purchase a gift for the mother, don't forget something for the father. Of course, their minds have one focus—successful labor and delivery. Eventually they will be able to focus and have a laugh or two as they bond with their newborn.

When the couple returns home, nothing could be more helpful than meals. You can go to the home to prepare a meal or bring frozen ones to store for the first week back at home. Another popular gesture is for a friend to organize a schedule and solicit meals from a circle of mutual friends. Then each person delivers their contribution to the family. If you choose this option, make sure to inquire about any food allergies or the family's favorite foods. Here's a good opportunity to have a special treat added for siblings.

Offers of babysitting older siblings or having children join yours for a play date allows the parents to bond with their newborn while big brother or big sister get to have some attention and fun.

If dad prefers to spend time with the children, you can offer to hold the newborn while mother takes a nice hot shower or has some quiet time in the presence of God to be refreshed. The offer of doing some household chores like washing dishes, doing a load or two of laundry, or vacuuming would lighten the load as well.

Above all, your loving support through a kind word or even just a cool, refreshing drink of water go a long way to helping a mother settle in as she sees you operating the "Golden Rule" of doing unto others as you'd have them do unto you.

CHAPTER 6

NATURAL CONCEPTION:

ACCEPTANCE OF GOD'S TIMING

For everything there is a season, and a time for every matter
under heaven:
a time to be born, and a time to die;
a time to plant, and a time to pluck up what was planted;
a time to kill, and a time to heal;
a time to break down, and a time to build up;
a time to weep, and a time to laugh;
a time to mourn, and a time to dance;
a time to cast away stones, and a time to gather stones
together;
a time to embrace, and a time to refrain from embracing;
a time to seek, and a time to lose;
a time to keep, and a time to cast away;
a time to tear; and a time to sew;
a time to keep silence; and a time to speak;
a time to love; and a time to hate;
a time of war; and a time of peace.
Ecclesiastes 3:1-8, ESV

"First comes love; then comes marriage; then comes the baby in the baby carriage." Do you remember that silly little rhyme? Most little kids use it as a way to tease and taunt their peers because of what they perceive to think about their lives. If you think about it, we often hear those same taunting words from friends and family members, as we get older. Our loved ones ask us 'Why aren't you dating or courting?' Then you meet someone. The courtship begins and then the next question becomes 'When are you getting married?' You then set a date for your wedding, have a beautiful ceremony to celebrate your union, to no later than the minute that you get back from your honeymoon, if not sooner, inquiring minds want to know 'When are you going to give me a little niece?' Whether you like it or not these are seeds being planted in your head. There is nothing wrong with having a desire to have children.

God gives us desires for a reason. It is an avenue through which He can get His purpose to be fulfilled. This is why He tells us to "Delight yourself in the Lord, and he will give you the desires of your heart." The thing that you have so much joy and passion for has purpose behind it. If you can recall your days practicing each and every stroke for the varsity relay or spending hour upon hour in rehearsing your lines for the upcoming production or how about fine tuning all the intricate details in the recipe for the debut of your very own restaurant, you didn't labor over the process because someone was forcing you to do it. When God downloads something into your heart, there is an organic and all-consuming desire to want to see it come to fruition. You are committed to the purpose behind the process.

Likewise God spends so much time knowing each and every detail of our lives. He does this because each and every child's life has a specific purpose for fulfilling his will. Just imagine as in Psalm 139:13-16, ESV perfectly describes of him:

For you formed my inward parts;You knitted me together in my mother's womb. I praise you, for I am fearfully and wonderfully made. Wonderful are your works; My soul knows it very well. My frame was not hidden form You, When I was being made in secret, Intricately woven in the depths of the earth. Your eyes saw my unformed substance; In your book were written, every One of them, The days that were formed for Me, When as yet there was none of them.

How awesome yet comforting is it to know that God takes great care and provides personal attention to our development from conception to birth, even to our last day on earth. So the whole time that you are hoping to have a child, remember that your child is being birthed for God's purpose here in this world. God's intricate details reach all the way down to the timing of it all.

Time has many definitions but when we relate it to purpose it all boils down to the period being measured during the process. Everything and everyone has a process to go through. It takes time with great patience; yet it is also necessary to endure going through the details of it. The details are what make the person; each person has a set of gifts, talents, and character. If we think about the process to produce a four-tiered wedding cake, it is not a fleeting task. The owner of a bakery or lead baker has to go through a lengthy and orderly process to get a flawless looking yet delectable treat. He or she either works alone or has multiple assistants that are calculating how many days to prep the fine molds, fondant decorations, and ultimate baking of the cakes to ultimately finalize the masterpiece. Rushing or skipping steps through the process could alter and affect the final product. I don't know about you but I have a serious sweet tooth; and I would hate if the cake that I ordered did not taste as expected because someone skimped on some of the ingredients or adjusted the oven's temperature in an attempt to speed up the baking process. You may think who would want to compromise their product. But it happens far too many times to those who are not willing to be patient to take care of the details. They are consumed with themselves because what they have before them is more important than the responsibility that has been given to them to complete the task.

We were born into being concerned with our own lives and not taking any thought to the purpose that others have been given. It is only through our walk with the Lord that He molds us into thinking less of ourselves and more of others. Our lives are just like that master handcrafted four-tiered cake. God is the owner and the lead baker; we are just the assistants carrying out His masterpiece.

Pregnancy has become trendy in pop culture. Thus, it has infiltrated even more into everyday conversations regarding the details of what the celebrity is wearing, who is decorating their baby's nursery, what the gender and the name of the baby is and a rundown of gifts the baby has received. It is in the cataloging of a stranger's life that we begin to draw comparisons with our own lives or try to duplicate what we believe is best and needed for our own family.

While celebrities are very much just people like you and I, people's security can be skewed when they focus on earthly goods versus eternity gain. When we get our focus off eternity, then we start making people, things, desires, and goals our god. God definitely works in us and there are always favorable outcomes for us; but it is not for our good but for His good pleasure. When He elevates us, strengthens our character or gives us tangible rewards, it is for His good pleasure. He is the one who blesses us because often times the things that are the most magnificent, we know we could not do in our own merit or strength. Ultimately He gets the glory, not us.

Will you trust Him even if you don't get pregnant next month or next year or whatever timetable you have mapped out? When we trust God, there is a peace that we receive because we know that He has our best interest at heart. Out of our peace, we receive joy because we found confidence in God and not only what He can do for us but just who He is in general.

There are times that many women express how they are not ready to get pregnant or take on the role of mother. They may be apprehensive or completely against having children because their conditions are not "perfect" or they "don't have it together." They would rather rely on their own intuition and insight to define the "perfect time" instead of asking God about building a family. Some women are naturally nurturing, some are naturally good in educating, and others are naturally inclined to encourage and inspire.

Regardless of what your natural giftings are, God does not entrust a child to you because He knows you have it all together. On the contrary, He knows how imperfect you are. He expects that you will not try to take His place, but that you will rely on the Holy Spirit to help you through the journey of motherhood. Accept your imperfections and trust that God is going to develop and complete the good work in you, so that you and your child lack nothing. You maybe thinking, 'What would you know about our hardship to conceive a child?' I may not have the experience of the delay to conceive a child;

however, I am quite familiar with the experience of being surprised by a pregnancy that I was not expecting—once when I was single and twice with my husband.

When my husband and I got married never did we think that we would conceive our first child together within nine months of marriage! We were definitely caught off guard. Immediately, I started my role as a new mom again very unsure of the future. I cried out to the Lord, 'You know our situation. Why now?!' In our minds, the timing for conceiving our first son couldn't have been more off. We were still in the process of working to successfully blend our family together.

It was a process in itself to come together as a man and wife, let alone both of us working on building a relationship with our children from previous relationships. Not to mention, we had also relocated from Atlanta back to my hometown in New York. Both my husband and I were looking for permanent employment, a residence to call our home, and my husband was in the process of solidifying his course schedule to return to college. He and I were invested in him finishing up school but also pursuing playing collegiate basketball with the hopes of being drafted.

I believed in his talent and felt such regret he had missed another opportunity. So, here we are pregnant, already have two children, no jobs and temporarily living with my parents. We were very hopeless, at first, not knowing how we were going to support our growing family. It was in that moment that our faith began to grow. Although looking back now, the shifts and changes were God's way of getting us back on the path towards His will. We saw how sovereign God is and that even though we didn't have what we wanted or thought we needed, He still provided and fulfilled the needs that were necessary to be worked out on our behalf.

Fast forward two years later, you would think that things would have gotten a lot better. Wrong! We were not only still living in my parents' house, but we were surprised with our second pregnancy. I cried out again, 'Lord, you have to be kidding me?' My husband had gained employment but then the company closed the site where he worked. I was working full-time at a Christian college; but we still were not able to afford to move out of my parents' home to raise our family. It seemed as though we were going in circles. We had talked about adding one or two children to our family. However, two more children within four years of marriage was more than we bargained for. During that time, we had no other choice but to trust God.

So you think to yourself, I've gotten on the right track. I graduated from college, was courted by my husband and we abstained from sex until marriage. We are good stewards over our finances; we serve in ministry; and we have the perfect home conducive for a family. Why are we not able to get pregnant? I am a firm believer that God opens and closes wombs. There are examples in the Bible for our reference of couples that desired a child, but were delayed the promise.

The two that most often come to mind are Sarah and Abraham and Rachel and Jacob. Both Sarah and Rachel were deeply loved by their husbands. Although both loved and served God, they did not conceive and birth a child for many years. Many laughed and did not believe that Sarah would give birth to a child, even Sarah herself was doubtful as she was past "childbearing age." Decades upon decades passed with more doubt than faith and without one pregnancy. However,

God graced her to give birth when many believed it was impossible. Likewise with Rachel, she did not conceive a child with Jacob for several years later. However, her sister Leah, who Jacob did not truly love, was more fertile than Rachel and gave Jacob children through deceit. Ultimately, through commitment and faithfulness Rachel and Jacob bore a child. .

In 1 Samuel 1: 5, we learn that the Lord closed Hannah's womb. In addition to her barrenness, she was talked about and teased which caused her much distress. It was to the point where it started to affect her relationship with her husband because he felt neglected and unloved. Not long after she prayed and stayed in peace regarding conception, it mentions in verse 19 of the Lord remembering her request and in due time, she conceived a son.

You can have all the right "ingredients" but if the timing is off; then nothing that you do is going to facilitate the process of getting pregnant. I know friends and acquaintances that have tracked their ovulation, increased sexual activity, spent several thousands of dollars for professional fertility assistance, and fasted and prayed for their child. However, they ultimately realized that it left them with a whole bunch of activity but no power. Yes, their prayers were heard. However, God does not always answer our prayers on our timetable. I believe that our willingness to trust Him through the process is one of the biggest keys to checking our heart in the matter.

We allow ourselves to have complete trust in the things that are calculated with our senses. However, we will never experience true freedom to trust Him if we continue to seek what we can see. The desire that God gave you was not done so in vain. There is purpose behind wanting to add a child to your family to nurture and raise. However, He never has put a time stamp on when we should get pregnant, or if we will have children. Motherhood comes in many different forms. Some of my friends have gone on to have a family, either biological or adopted, while some continue to wait.

When you think about the process that it takes for a flower to bloom, it does not happen overnight. Before anything, the seed is not just sown in any ground. The soil is inspected for the proper nutrients and supplements because if it is poor quality, it will choke the seed and there will be no root to produce growth. It then needs to be planted at the right time because the details of the environment could be a hindrance to the growth and development of the flower. After the seed is sown into good ground, there is tender care and attention to ensuring that it has all the necessities like light, water, and nutrients free from weeds that could choke the growth process.

You have to consider the desire for a child that you and your husband have as a seed. The ultimate purpose is very precious and delicate. You have to ensure that you are allowing your purpose-driven flower to grow and mature in good ground. So now is the perfect time to evaluate your heart, your earthly soil. Your heart has to be clean and available for the Lord to use you. Have you allowed Him to start the process of renewing your heart in areas that are not pleasing or proper for edifying His kingdom? Have you become so consumed with your own needs and wants that you are drawing back from His very presence from your life? Have you pursued and sought out what He expects from you in this season of your life? Or have you allowed man-made visions and expectations to become your idol? God could be speaking to you about building your family. However, if He is not leading the process or if your focus is more on the gift than on Him, how can He entrust you with the child, that is ultimately His, when you are too busy to acknowledge Him through it all. God wants all of you, including your plans and dreams. Once you allow Him to have His rightful place, He can start to renew and replenish the proper nutrients in your spirit so that the good timing for fertilization fulfills its purpose.

CHAPTER 7

NATURAL CHILDBEARING:

EMPLOYING ONE'S

CORRESPONDING ACTION

Desire without knowledge is not good,
and whoever makes haste with his feet misses his way.

Proverbs 19:2 , ESV

It was clear to me that repeating the same birth plan or investing in the same childbirth education that I had used during my first pregnancy would be foolish. If I wanted a different result, I would have to change not only my mind, but my actions to follow suit. Pregnancy is very demanding on the entire being of the mom-to-be. Hormones drive the physical, mental, and emotional health of a woman. When I was pregnant with my daughter, there was one rule in my head: I was allowed to eat whatever I wanted, whenever I wanted. I was coached and received affirmation from friends and acquaintances that it was fine to consume my cravings of high fatty and sugary intoxicating foods to my heart's content. I believe my family endorsed my food choices out of pity; but there was no food or beverage that could fill the void of the extreme loneliness I felt. The unspeakable joy in my heart, which I later found in my life, was only filled by my Heavenly Father.

Pregnant or not, it is important to maintain a healthy, balanced diet. But it is even more important to make healthy food choices during your pregnancy. It is through your food choices that you are setting the foundation for your baby's health while building and maintaining your own health. Your body is working overtime to house and provide the ultimate nutrients necessary for prime fetal growth. The amount of weight gain not only has an effect on your baby's birth weight but her overall long-term health. You are not eating for two, but it is necessary to maintain a healthy environment for baby by eating 300 additional calories.

A variety of fruits, vegetables, grains, and protein should be included in your daily meal plan. In addition, it is very important to take a daily prenatal vitamin so that your body receives necessary essential minerals and vitamins such as folic acid, iron, copper, Vitamin D and Vitamin B. Although our budget was extremely tight, I made it work to eat a balanced diet without breaking the bank. During my first pregnancy what helped us tremendously was receiving WIC. As mentioned my husband did not have a permanent full-time job. Therefore, we did not have any insurance and had to sign up for Medicaid. WIC allowed me to receive a variety of healthy foods for free. Most states allow you to shop not only at major supermarkets but farmer's markets as well. This meant I was able to get healthy organic fruits and vegetables. It wasn't an ideal situation, but provision was there when we temporarily needed it.

In addition to fueling your body with the proper nutrients, it is also important to maintain or start implementing low impact physical fitness. It is suggested that you not take on a rigorous workout routine, if working out was never part of your regular lifestyle prior to pregnancy. However, this should not be a reason not to implement or deter you from making healthy choices.

Over the last several years, I have not been consistent in maintaining a physical fitness routine. But during my pregnancies, I pushed myself to implement some cardio into my day. I would take long walks at the park or at the mall with my family; at work I would take walks around campus; and I would park towards the back of the parking lot when I would go to the grocery store. The benefits are endless when you make some adjustments to implement exercise into your lifestyle while pregnant. To state the obvious, you will gain less weight and as a result have more energy throughout your pregnancy and potentially recover more quickly after birth.

Throughout labor and delivery your stamina is going to be essential. So, training your body during your pregnancy will get you prepared for the duration of your baby's birth. Water aerobic and yoga are known to bring relief if you have back issues during your pregnancy. Stretching definitely helped relieve my aching muscles after a long day at work or was a great start to my day after a night of slumber. In addition, exercising could reduce leg swelling because of improving blood flow throughout the body. As, I mentioned you can implement an actual gym routine or making small adjustments to your everyday routine to better your health and the health of your baby.

In an earlier chapter, I covered the importance of staying in peace during pregnancy. I am now going to expand and discuss how it correlates with labor. Your uterus is one of the most important organs during your pregnancy. It is a muscle that facilitates your baby going through the start to the end of the birthing process. In sum, the uterus works to push your baby down and out through the birth canal. Like any muscle, proper knowledge of how it functions and understanding your part in it working properly is extremely important. Yes, we have a part to play in the way it operates. Your uterus like any organ, system or cell needs adequate hydration and nutrients.

When your body is working overtime, you lose vital sodium and electrolytes. These components need to be restored to your cells, so that your uterus, the muscle, is functioning optimally. If you get dehydrated, this leads to more pain because reduction in fluids outside of the cells causes nerve endings to be pinched. So to avoid the unnecessary stress to the muscle, replenish it with liquids such as a sports drink or even better coconut water. Coconut water is naturally full of electrolytes. You can also provide your uterus with the proper nutrients by eating small super foods that will give it a boost, such as mixed nuts and dried fruit, hummus and carrots, green smoothies, to name a few. Super packed energy foods give you the boost that you need for the entirety of your birth process.

Another component to your uterus working properly during the birthing process is relaxation and breathing. The blood flow to the uterus is blocked off during contractions. The blood flow is blocked off for longer amounts of time and occurs more frequently as the contractions become longer and closer together. The decrease in oxygen to the uterus may trigger pain. Relaxation provides the uterus an improvement in efficiently getting oxygen to mother and baby. Another reason it is so important to be relaxed and at peace is because the body naturally releases hormones based on our emotions.

Oxytocin is also known as a love hormone; but in childbirth it is an essential part of the success in labor and delivery of the baby. Oxytocin is naturally released during labor. However, it is slowed down and sometimes non-existent when fear and stress are present. When fear and stress are present, your body releases a commonly known hormone called adrenaline. Adrenaline is known as "fight or flight" hormone. The hormone is released typically in response to stress and fear. Adrenaline is necessary in childbirth as it provides the woman with a rush of energy and also helps with the reflex of the baby being released. However, too much adrenaline can impede or completely stall labor, which equates to a longer and sometimes more painful childbirth.

In an effort to balance the adrenaline hormone, endorphins are released. This is why learning natural birthing exercises is so important. It allows the body to release more endorphins, which is natural and more effective to get calm and get relief from any pain. It is ultimately the body's natural morphine which will decrease the pain. My last childbirth experience felt like pain was almost non-existent. It was better described as intense pressure. If I had to compare it to anything, I would say it was similar to working your biceps. With the right size weight, working the muscles correctly, using proper form and breathing correctly, you will feel pressure and the more you work it only slight pain. However, it will not be excruciating or unbearable pain. The uterus is also a muscle that has to be given the same attention and care to work efficiently during labor.

It is going to be important that during your pregnancy you that you take the necessary measures to prepare yourself for childbirth and postpartum care. I would suggest that you and your husband interchangeably educate yourself on childbirth and understanding medical interventions. Some may be confused that a natural childbirth advocate would encourage researching medical interventions. However, I make the suggestion because you want to know the effects that it could potentially have on you and your child during delivery. Healthy pregnant women are very capable of having a natural birth.

Some medical professionals will suggest, provide, or bully parents-to-be with unnecessary information. Bully? Why would my doctor do that? If you decide to receive prenatal care from an OB-GYN, this practitioner is going give you treatment based on their medical training. Doctors are trained from a scientific perspective, which may not acknowledge that childbirth is a natural process of life. Some doctors are going to evaluate and make decisions to "treat" what will ultimately lead to possible unnecessary interventions.

Interventions such as inductions, C-sections, and use of forceps are too frequently the alternatives for doctors who use the "textbook approach" to care. However, the number of women given these interventions could be significantly reduced with proper education and care for the parents-to-be. Hospitals are ultimately a business and medical professionals are there to make sure that the business operates effectively.

I'm not saying that medical interventions are never needed. However, I am against making decisions that are based on fear.

You need to know your rights so that hospital policies, procedures, and doctor's views don't impede your birth plan. This is why it is so important to be educated about your options from the start. There are a variety of prenatal care plans you can receive. You can receive care from an OB/GYN or a midwife. You can decide to labor in a hospital, birthing center, or at home. You can decide to have a doula or support from your husband and/or loved one present during your childbirth.

After you interview and select your doctor, midwife and/or doula, you will want to decide how you are going to manage your childbirth. If you decide you want to have a natural childbirth, start researching the method that will work for you. I enjoyed my entire labor and delivery experiences with my last two pregnancies. You may think, 'What type of woman enjoys childbirth?' This woman right here! I have gone through three different types of childbirth classes. My first childbirth class was really not a natural childbirth course. It was more an overview of pregnancy, childbirth, and postpartum care, that just so happened to touch on Lamaze.

Information was included in my "Congratulations packet" given to me at my doctor's appointment that confirmed my pregnancy. In my 21-year-old mind, it was convenient because it was being offered at the hospital I was delivering at so it had to be right. I didn't know there were other courses and methods. After I realized that Lamaze didn't work for me, I decided to do a little more research when I got confirmation of our first son. While searching I came across the Bradley Method and Hypnobirthing.

After finding a local educator and exchanging messages about the curriculum, I registered for an intensive course for second time parents. I didn't have an option on the course track because I was too close to my due date to complete either of the regular courses. The first night my husband and I didn't know what to expect when we pulled up to a luxury home in an affluent community.

I definitely caught my husband off guard as he questioned what I had gotten us into. He thought we were going to attend a course at a hospital. After we laughed it off, we entered the home where we were immediately eased by the instructor's kind and relaxed personality. She was confident and transferred her confidence in her curriculum. She convinced my reluctant husband and myself and made us confident in the material. I can recall I was very content with my labor in delivery.

On a Sunday morning, I woke up to some slight discomfort but shrugged it off as I thought my son was "stretching out in an uncomfortable position." Little did I know that I was in labor. I eventually got out of the bed and went to cook breakfast for my daughter who was already awake. Yes, I was cooking breakfast through contractions. After tending to my daughter, I noticed that the "stretching of my son" did not ease up. So, I began to time what I then started to identify as contractions. The contractions became more regular so I called my husband who was at work and my parents who were almost at church. After everyone arrived home, an hour and a half after waking up, we headed to the hospital to check-in. The nurses and midwife were ready for me. However, the nurses laughed at me because they didn't believe I was in active labor because I didn't look distraught. They were certainly surprised when they examined me and announced that I was 6 centimeters dilated. I shocked them even more another hour and half later when my water broke and was dilated at 10 centimeters and ready to push. My son leapt into the world four and half hours from the first contraction at home.

We were loved and were instantly engaged with the Bradley Method because the instructor gave some basic information about the effects that fear plays in pregnancy and childbirth. It gave me immediate confirmation on the convictions that I had all along. The three-session course involved more curriculum but also practical exercises that could be used in the birthing room. What I loved and appreciate to this day is how the course was a source of bonding between my husband and me. The Bradley Method is unique because both the mother and the husband together play an active part in the birthing process. It allowed me to tune into an awareness of my body while using natural breathing and relaxation techniques the entire time.

Although I was able to have an unmedicated natural childbirth using the Bradley Method, I wanted a little more to my experience when I found out that we were pregnant again two years after with our second son. Although I was able to endure, I wasn't present and completely relaxed during my contractions. Even though I had mastered the breathing techniques, my body did not reflect that I was in a state of peace. I wanted to fully surrender my mind, body, and spirit to the Lord. This time I would take the necessary steps to enroll in not just the course, but the training course to become a Hypnobirthing course instructor.

The theory of Hypnobirthing and the Bradley Method are very similar. The difference is that Hypnobirthing teaches birthing women and their support partners non-pharmacological strategies, such as relaxation, meditation, and visualization that allow the body to birth naturally without restrictions. Hypnosis has received a bad wrap; especially from the Christian community. Hypnobirthing is a derivative of hypnosis. Some mistake or assume that it is not of God because they believe hypnotists have a person under their control. Actually, people are hyper attentive and are doing things of their free will. You are in a "daydreaming" state but fully conscious and able to tune out distractions.

At first I was unsure about the training course, I didn't want to do anything that contradicted my Christian principles. However, I was able to be at peace once I concluded that I was being hypersensitive and nothing was contradicting the Word of God. There always the possibility of coming across someone who does not share your beliefs or even those who are a part of a New Age or Atheist group. However, the Holy Spirit will speak to you and reveal the intent of the matter.

As long as everything you do and say lines up with the Word of God, nothing else matters. After taking the four-day course, I came out pretty excited and confident about the material. I was looking forward to birthing my baby. When I returned home, I started practicing my breathing each day and using visualization to get me into a state of relaxation. Instead of listening and repeating the affirmations that came along with the course like, "I relax and my baby relaxes," I meditated on scripture like "You keep him in perfect peace whose mind is stayed on you, because he trusts in you." I looked over scriptures concerning peace and trust in God.

I also created a playlist of music to listen to when I started labor. I selected songs that would become my anchor to get into a relaxed state throughout the birthing experience. It was explained that music has the profound affect of allowing people to get energized or to the extreme of falling asleep. The variation of sounds evokes different feelings. It is important that if you are going to use music, the music has slow tempo. I knew immediately that I would intertwine worship music into my relaxation techniques. Up tempo songs with bass, drums, or screaming would distract me. I selected songs that I knew would bring me into the presence of the Lord. I knew that was a place of peace and rest. So, I selected one of my now all time favorites, "Be Still" and "Tides" by Bethel Music and others like "There is A River" by Mary Alessi and "Closer/Wrap Me In Your Arms" by William McDowell. The atmosphere in your room has to be drenched with peace.

Music can be influential but so can the people who you choose to be in your room. When deciding who is going to be in your birthing room, make sure that they are going to add value by staying peaceful, speaking in a calm voice, and advocating for your needs that match your birth plan. If you know that the person is going to be a distraction by being loud, emotional, and negative, then I would think twice about inviting them to be in the room. You want to make sure that you have little to no distractions. I would suggest no more than three or four people.

It was the day of my grandmother's 98th birthday and everyone was on pins and needles as to whether I would have my baby boy Cayden that day. I was determined to make her luncheon. I knew that these were memories that I couldn't get back; not to mention my grandmother was not getting any younger. Concern was obvious on some faces as they thought that any moment, I would need to be rushed to the hospital. I chose to continue to talk, laugh, and enjoy some yummy cake. Yes, I knew I was on the very onset of labor but I wasn't going to stop staying relaxed and in peace. We even went to a friend's graduation party following. I knew that as long as I had my hospital bag that I was only a ride away.

It was approximately 2:00 am and after having a midnight bathroom break, I knew I was in active labor. I alerted my husband who started getting everything in order. I reverted back to my usual warm shower relaxation technique until my contractions were close enough for us to go to the hospital. We decided to go to the hospital after a few hours because we didn't want to chance a home or car birth. After all, "they" say your labor is shorter after your first childbirth. My birth with Azaria was 10 hours long; my birth with Caleb was four and a half hours; so we were all predicting it to be significantly less. I continued on with my slow breathing to the rhythm of my playlist.

We arrived at the hospital and I was greeted with the same welcome we received when I was in labor with Caleb. Nurses didn't think that I was in active labor. However, they were mistaken when they confirmed that I was five centimeters dilated. But they dismissed my progress because I was not in distress. As I rolled around on the birthing ball, I noticed that it had been five hours of being labor. At that point, I had to make a decision not to look at the clock again because it would be a distraction and break my peace. I continued on as I dismissed the commentary of the nurses regarding my progress. After another comment about the baby resisting descent during each contraction, I told him softly, "It's okay Cayden; there is nothing to be afraid of. You can come now."

Within an hour, my look as they had described as being on a vacation turned into a look of focused attention to each slow breathe. Up until then I was concerned about the birth breathing. I had been practicing it at home but I didn't know how breathing him down without using the pushing technique would work. When it was time to meet our little boy and my contractions got closer and closer together, I started to panic after I attempted the birth breathing. The quick burst of fear that overwhelmed my body transitioned to the first real pain that I felt.

Channing and the nurse immediately got in my face and pulled me back through words of affirmation and massage. I then rejected the fear that was trying to take over and returned back to peace. It was then I allowed my body to work the way it was supposed to and we met our baby boy shortly after.

CHAPTER 8

SWEET EXPOSURE:

PREPARING FOR BREASTFEEDING

For you formed my inward parts;
You knitted me together in my Mother's womb.
I praise you, for I am fearfully and wonderfully made,
Wonderful are your works;
My soul know it very well.
Psalm 139:13-14, ESV

Mothers want to give their babies the very best, especially during the early and crucial developmental years. Although breastfeeding has regained popularity with moms, the origin of this trend to provide a healthy start, dated back centuries ago. This is the reason I encourage all moms to consider breastfeeding for feeding their child, even if their forebears never breastfed their babies. Often I heard people say, "I don't know about breastfeeding my child. My mom, my grandmothers, or aunts didn't breastfed their children." How often are you not aware of things that occurred or did not happen in your family's history? It is not unusual that conversations and family stories are not openly shared.

This is the very reason that we cannot live our lives being subject to people's opinions or words. Our families are

131

typically the first source of our education, where we gain learned behavioral and cultural norms. However, our families are subject to fail us because they are not perfect. They provide us the best foundation that may have been available to them. However, even the most educated families do not always have the best information. This is why it is so important to seek wisdom for yourself. In fact, nutrition is an area where earlier generations may not have been as informed about a nutritious diet.

Breast milk provides the very best nutrients for your child. It provides all the necessary vitamins, minerals, and even antibodies to aid in the growth and development of your child, as well as the protection of their immune system. This is why I strongly encourage mothers to try nursing as the primary source for feeding their babies, even if it's for a short period of time. There is a reason why so many companies and manufacturers of formula are trying to duplicate breast milk. Though there are great attempts made year after year, there has been no success in creating an exact duplicate of what many refer to as "liquid gold." God created breast milk with so many unique properties, even down to the taste of the milk.

Aside from giving my child a healthy start, I gained an authentic love for breastfeeding right from the start. It allowed me to instantly receive a deeper level of intimacy between me and my child. Breastfeeding is not just a means to an end to provide your baby nutrition; breastfeeding also enhances your relationship with your child. In the early days of my children's lives, breastfeeding was our hidden communication with one another. There were little to no words spoken, but the bond was almost tangible. Ever heard of sex unifying husband and wife? The same oxytocin that is released during sex is the same chemical released during breastfeeding.

I listen to so many moms who chose to formula feed their child mention how bottle feeding is so much easier. Now don't get me wrong, every mom has her own preference and routine that works for her. However, the fact that you don't have to sterilize your breast before and after seems like a great bonus to me. Not to mention, your breast milk is available immediately for consumption and always at the perfect temperature, without prepping or measuring. If there is any inconvenience it might be the delay of finding a comfortable place when you are outside of the home or wrestling with a difficult bra strap. Nonetheless, you do not have to spend a lengthy time to prepare your baby's feeding session.

Breastfeeding is also a way to provide comfort to your baby who is teething, hurt, or upset. There are medical professionals who will advise you not to use your breasts as a pacifier. But these are typically professionals who are not educated fully on the purpose of breastfeeding. Your child early on is learning social cues such as trust, acceptance, and love. Mothers are emotionally and behaviorally influenced by active oxytocin and prolactin hormones that make you more inclined to be protective and have a more unified bond to your child. These all are cues that are learned, instinctively or over the course of time, in the relationship between mother and child and breastfeeding just enhances it.

Breastfeeding may not come easy for many moms. There are some moms, who may run into challenges with breastfeeding, but others may have little to no issues at all. There may even be moms who find that breastfeeding is just not for them; and others who find that breastfeeding is the best thing ever. And there are a rare, small percentage of moms who are unable to produce breast milk or their baby was born with an anatomical deformity that would make it almost impossible to breastfeed without medical intervention. Some moms just don't have a desire for any particular reason at all and some who feel uncomfortable with the thought of their baby latching onto their breast.

I am often asked by moms-to-be, "How can I prepare to breastfeed my baby?" There are two factors that will be influential for having a successful breastfeeding experience: faith and patience. Our bodies are designed to carry a growing baby; in addition, our bodies are designed to lactate. Many at some point in their breastfeeding experience, question whether they are able to produce breast milk at all or whether or not they are producing enough or even doubt the quality of milk. How awesome is God's handiwork!? It is only He that could take such time, detail, and creativity to know and meet the needs of not only of a woman, but her child.

God is the same Creator who designed our organs and each working system to function in harmony and sustain us through life. We never question our ability to breathe. Instead, we take each breathe in and exhale out without even thinking about it. Nevertheless, we often doubt our body's ability to

NADRA DYAN COHENS

lactate. I like to relate breast milk as an authentic example of our faith in God. We are not able to see the production and the mechanics of it all. Yet behind the scenes, your brain, each hormone, each cell, and tissue, is steadily working together to produce milk that is specifically designed with the necessary nutrients and antibodies just for your baby alone. You can't see the process that it takes to be produced and you don't know the exact amount that your baby is consuming; yet it is available and your baby is able to thrive and grow in good health. You have to trust that your body is working just as it was designed to.

If your baby's pediatrician isn't raising any concerns about his weight and he is having an adequate amount of wet and dirty diapers, then you can rest assured that your baby is getting the appropriate amount of milk. You have to take a stand and use faith in the God that formed your inward parts.

There will be plenty of opportunities along the way when you may doubt your body's ability to supply milk. The most skillful and veteran breastfeeding moms have had their share of doubt. In fact, I had an opportunity to allow myself to be fearful of my milk supply being negatively impacted. I made the wrong decision of scheduling a contract job on the same day I was going out of town to assist my best friend at her speaking engagement.

Ever have that moment when you feel like you can take on the world? Well, I did in the moment and it jeopardized our travel plans, my peace, and my milk supply. Since my contract job started in the morning, I had no time to pump before we jetted to the airport to make our flight. This was a huge no-no and I always advise my own clients to nurse or express on baby's demand or every three to four hours. So, needless to say, I was extremely engorged.

The added fluid pressure and blocked milk ducts turned into a virus called mastitis. While trying to nurse myself back to wellness, my symptoms kept getting worse and worse even while pumping on and off and putting heat compresses on my breasts.

Although I am a certified lactation counselor, I have a handful of professionals who I stay connected to network and brainstorm. I called one for input on how I could self-treat until I got back home. Though she was giving me solid and accurate information, I could have allowed fear to set in because ultimately I was putting my milk supply at risk. However, I got my emotions under control and took one hour at a time. I was able to get myself into 100% health without any medical interventions.

The moral of the story is that there is always be unexpected scenarios and breastfeeding is no exception to presenting those instances. You have to not allow your emotions to rule you because it can tempt you to make hasty decisions that are not in your best interest.

In addition to building up your spiritual muscles, you can increase wisdom by reading literature on breastfeeding such as "The Nursing Mother's Companion" by Kathleen Huggins. There isn't anything that you have to physically prepare to breastfeed your baby. However, if you read and learn about how breast milk is produced and how to sustain your supply, it will help you to understand the importance of allowing your baby to do such things as feed on demand.

Life's struggles and most painful moments can try and damper the most precious times. There are some women who voice their distaste in breastfeeding because those same women have gone through some very traumatic experiences such as childhood sexual abuse or rape at some point during their life. Whether they have spent years suppressing the event(s) or have tried to seek closure, the thought of breastfeeding can open up some old wounds. Ultimately, this leads some women to either relive and endure or reject the option to breastfeed their baby completely. For those women who are creating battles in their mind, I completely understand. I was one of those women.

Although I had a desire to breastfeed all of my children, the war in my head didn't stop when I got pregnant and had my babies. If anything, the sexual trauma reared its ugly head from time to time because I had not admitted to the abuse that I endured when I was a child or the rape that occurred in college. It was years and years of fighting shame because, a brief period of my youth, I was confused about my identity due to my sexual nature being awakened so early and the perverted seeds that were planted. It was also years of low self-esteem and hating my body that kept the secret brewing.

I was determined not to let it affect breastfeeding my first baby; but it was on my terms and in my own strength. There were times I would feel uncomfortable, violated, and would retreat when a medical professional would touch me. I remembered there were times that I had to encourage myself that it was for the health and benefit of my own baby. However, after fifteen months of fighting the memories resurfacing from time to time, I self weaned her because it had gotten to be too much. Many people praised me for breastfeeding for that long; however little did they know that the end was for selfish reasons. It wasn't until I actually voiced the traumatic events and sought healing that I began to feel whole. Yes, I verbalized and was transparent to my husband and a close friend. However, complete healing and restoration only came from the Lord Jesus Christ. There was no family member, no professional counselor that was going to be able to take that sting away. If this resonates with you, I admonish and encourage you to seek out a close friend, family member, or professional counselor that you trust and has your same Christian beliefs to share.

If for any other reason, allow this to be an opportunity for the devil to no longer have a foothold in your life. I knew I had to seek peace and healing when he was taunting me by using fear of my past to dictate the decisions I had to make concerning my family. I had to surrender my past, my hurts, and my feelings to the Lord. It was in this place that healing was made available because I no longer held on to the defense of self-protection. However, I would not and still to this day do not stop renewing my mind. I held tight to the sweet words of the Lord, "...be attentive to my words; incline your ear to my sayings. Let them not escape from your sight; keep them within your heart. For they are life to those who find them, and healing to all their flesh." (Proverbs 4:20-22, ESV). Don't let the enemy twist and manipulate what your body was designed by God Himself to do; you were created to birth and provide the very best nourishment for your baby.

You have to take into consideration that breastfeeding is a relationship that has to grow. Every relationship takes time and patience – breastfeeding is no exception. In the early days, new mothers are thrown into a crash course of learning baby's cries that vary from wanting comfort to nourishment, juggling household and family demands to postpartum hormonal flare-ups, to trying to find sleep in between everything else. Your baby is also going through a bit of culture shock as well. Life outside of the womb is very overwhelming and their senses are over stimulated. You are not just working together with your husband and family. But you also have to keep in mind that you are going to work with your baby. Since he is a baby, there is going to be less reciprocation and more giving on your end. But whether you are breastfeeding or not, you have to ask the Lord to give you strength to be more compassionate and giving.

If you haven't already learned with regards to your marriage, you will quickly be thrown into boot camp of having a servant's heart. A servant doesn't consider his needs or wants but considers the needs of others. Although my love language is acts of service, my servant heart's tank can get low at times, especially when my "to do" list is too long. When I start getting weary and tempted to voice complaints, I review the Word about how Jesus served His disciples and those He encountered. I get humbled quickly when I realize that Christ our Savior was a servant and He didn't always consider Himself, instead thought of others.

Breastfeeding is not just a new task for you, but for your baby too. What is awesome is that babies have an innate ability to suckle at the breast. His keen senses will also allow him to find a food source. However, you will need to seek and pursue peace so that you are in a calm state each time you decide to breastfeed your baby. Your ability to stay relaxed and calm will help calm his nerves so that he is not anxious when latching onto your breast. If your baby is not latched on correctly, just try again. The breastfeeding relationship will develop in its time. It is key that your level of patience is consistent, as it can have an affect on your milk supply. The less patient you are, the more likely you are to rush your baby to latch on, which presents opportunities early on for an incorrect latch onto the breast. In these moments, moms complain of pain but for the majority of the time it is because the baby is not latched on correctly. There may be some discomfort in the initial days. However, breastfeeding is not supposed to hurt. You should not be in discomfort for very long either. A correct latch is not only going help you feel comfortable, but it will also maximize your milk supply. It is important that you seek as much assistance right after your baby's birth. There are professionals available in the hospital, birthing center, WIC offices, pediatric offices, and sometimes in the comfort of your home to guide you through the blurry lines and potential "cries" from you and your baby.

Support is also crucial in developing a good breastfeeding relationship. Many of your hours and days are going to be dedicated to breastfeeding your baby. Some babies will nurse every two to three hours, but don't be surprised if your baby is going to nurse every hour on the hour. Your ability to have one person or a support team will make all the difference in the world. When people ask if there is anything they can do for you, humbly take their offer. You would be surprised at the difference it will make to have someone even do everyday chores such as cooking a meal, folding some clothes, or entertaining older children.

It can be a game-changer when pays a visit so that you can take a shower or have some adult conversation. There is no task too small or too big. In my own personal experience, I have given my time to friends during the early postpartum days as a baby shower gift. Couples are relieved and excited because this is something that benefits the family, especially if they already have little ones as well as the new baby. Your ability to have your schedule lightened during the early days, will allow you to have focused time on your baby's feeding cues, learning their temperament, and knowing what works and what does not. However, it is also going to be crucial to seek out a positive circle of mothers to encourage and support you.

The same principles that applied during pregnancy need to stay intact during postpartum days when you are the most vulnerable. You want to have encouraging women speaking life into you, and serving you with tender, loving care. Whether you are a new mom-to-be or a veteran mom, I always advise having a lactation counselor or consultant saved on your 'Favorites List' on your phone. Just as each pregnancy is unique in nature, likewise is your breastfeeding relationship with your baby. With all of my personal experience and my certification as a lactation consultant, there have been times when I have brainstormed, bounced ideas, and tips off consultant friends.

I remember with my first son it was days after his birth that my milk came in and I was completely engorged. I had no breastfeeding issues during the early days of postpartum with my first child. I couldn't understand why I was not getting any relief after nursing; and why it was difficult for him to latch on. It was in the wee hours of the night where I would find relief in the information that a lactation consultant friend gave me by identifying the problem and guiding me on the phone about how to eliminate the fluid pressure that was causing the blockage. I knew that the issue prior to my conversation was not the end to breastfeeding days. However, there are many women who leave the hospital to return home and willingly give up because help was not sought out. While you are researching and interviewing pediatricians for your baby, start the same process and select one or two lactation counselors or consultants to have available after you return home and enter your breastfeeding journey. There will be plenty of opportunities to use her service because there will be times when you may need questions answered when you return to work or run into issues later in your breastfeeding journey.

Speaking of the journey, along the way it is important that while you are taking care of your baby's needs that you do not neglect yourself. This is easier said then done sometimes. However, it will be important to make sure that you are still maintaining a healthy and balanced diet. Your diet is more critical now as your body is transitioning from carrying a growing fetus to producing and maintaining your baby's milk supply. This is still demanding work on your body. Your body will always provide your baby what he needs regardless of what you eat or drink. Ensuring that you are consuming an adequate amount of calories will be necessary to sustain energy and activity throughout the day. It will be helpful to continue snacking throughout the day. But now more than ever, it will be important to have snacks nearby that you can access and eat while balancing a little one.

To stay well-hydrated, make sure that you have a water bottle or two throughout the house. If it is accessible to you throughout the day, it will be easy to maintain hydration. While in the hospital nurses may want to aggressively make you drink tons of water. It is indeed very important to stay hydrated, but it is more important to drink to your thirst as opposed to consuming a certain number of ounces during the day. This will help take some of the pressure off.

It will also be just as important to have time out of the house. Although your baby is young and you may not be able to part from your baby for long, it is key to get some fresh air.

It's amazing how a walk around the block helps maintain your sanity. Schedule alone and quiet time to keep you at peace. In the same vein, as much as you need to recharge yourself mentally, it is all the important to recharge yourself spiritually. You may find it hard to have quiet time/ prayer alone.

You will need to get creative. You may not be able to have unlimited time with the Lord but you can rearrange your schedule for Him. This will be the time that you can introduce your baby to the Lord by having quiet time with her. Another option is having your quiet time when your husband is spending quality time with the baby. Let the Lord continue to lead you on how to spend time with Him. You may feel apprehensive about leaving your child or may feel like time is not available, but it is really crucial to find the time. You will not be any good to your baby or the rest of your family if you do not invest in making sure that your peace and rest is maintained.

EPILOGUE

I firmly believe that my pregnancy, labor, and delivery were a testament to my proactive faith and implementation of the wisdom and knowledge that I applied. Does this mean that a woman who chooses to have a medicated birth doesn't have a firm foundation of faith and trust in God? Or better does a woman who endures a long, strenuous and/or complicated labor experience that because she has less faith? Absolutely not! The only requirement that God gives us as believers is to love, trust, and obey Him.

God did not promise that we wouldn't go through trials and tribulations. Quite the contrary, He prepared us for when we do face trials and tribulations. "Count it all joy, my brothers, when you meet trials of various kinds, for you know that the testing of your faith produces steadfastness. And let steadfastness have its full effect that you may be perfect and complete, lacking in nothing. If you need wisdom, ask our generous God, and he will give it to you" (James 4:2-4). He is still God and is there for his daughter in a short and painless childbirth just like he remains the same for his daughter in an emergency C-section. Life is so unpredictable. The one thing that remains constant is God and if we can walk through the trial, He can provide comfort and peace through it all and some day provide that same comfort to someone else (2 Corinthians 1:3-4).

Lord, I pray for my dear sister in Christ who received your inspired words that were given just for her. I pray that in receiving your word that you were purifying her heart and leaving your wisdom on good ground. We believe that You are not a God who is a respecter of persons. We believe You will never leave us nor forsake us, especially now going into a new season as a mother. Our hope is in You, Lord, that your hand of protection is upon this new mother to be and her child. I pray that You are imparting sound wisdom and that she will receive revelation pertaining to each detail of her pregnancy and birthing.

I thank You that You have prepared the right medical team to be over her prenatal care, labor, and delivery. You have given them insight into every need that is required to provide Your daughter the very best care. I thank You, Lord, that You are keeping her in perfect peace as her mind is fixed on You. I believe You are imparting a new revelation of Your plan for her.

I believe that her light will shine that all men will draw near to You because of Your love that will be sown. I thank You for complete health in her life and in her child's life; and that You will continue to fulfill Your will for her life.

We receive it and declare it as so and it is in Jesus' name that we pray. Amen.

Made in the USA
Lexington, KY
04 July 2015